FAMILY KEEPSAKE QUILTS

Capturing Treasured Memories in Cloth

by Vivian Howell Ritter

Leman
Publications
Inc.

This book is dedicated to my families—the Howells, Hughes, McGregors, and Ritters.

Vivian Ritter

Project Director: Bonnie Leman
Book Design and Production: Kathryn Wagar Wright
Drawings: Marla Gibbs Stefanelli
Photography: Mellisa A. Karlin, black and white photos and color photos on pages 25, 31, and 38; Jerry DeFelice, all other color photos unless otherwise noted.

▲

Contents

▲

Introduction

A big reunion of my husband's family at Lake Canton, Oklahoma, was the beginning of making family keepsake quilts for me. When I made a family tree quilt to present to my in-laws, Cora and Glenn Ritter, at that celebration, I had no idea that it would be the first of many quilts I would make for family members. But as I learned, when you make one family quilt, you may end up making several more.

That first family tree quilt led to one for my own parents. Then, of course, I had to make my children's family tree. Then the 50th wedding anniversaries began: first my in-laws, then my parents, next the aunt for whom I was named, and a favorite aunt and uncle of my husband—the family through which we first met. How could I not make a quilt for them? And of course there were the baby quilts for the newest members of the family, my children's graduation quilts, and my sister's 50th birthday quilt.

Most of the quilts I have made for these special events

Left, "Happy Birthday, Gramma," 34" x 34". Center, "Happy 50th," 60" x 60". Right, "Birthday Quilt," 24" x 24". These quilts were made by the author.

have been made for non-quilters. I know that my husband's parents would have appreciated a lovely bed quilt for their 50th wedding anniversary. But if I had made a bed quilt worthy of winning a national contest and given it to them, I don't think they would have been nearly as thrilled as when they walked into a room and saw their album quilt hanging on the wall. It is full of wonderful messages from family friends, some from people they had not heard from for years. The quilt is a simple-to-piece, machine-made quilt. It might not catch the eye of a judge at a quilt show, but it now hangs by their front door, and all who enter there are invited to read its loving messages.

Special-occasion and family-history quilts will probably be cherished like no other type of quilt you ever make. They may not take the blue ribbon at your state fair and they may not be your masterpiece quilts, but they will most likely be the quilts that will be cared for and will be passed from generation to generation. "This quilt was given to Grandma Rebecca on her wedding day by her mother."

A family heritage quilt does not have to be elaborate or difficult to make. It can be the simplest Nine Patch crib quilt for a new grandson, and because you have embroidered his name, birth date, and your name on it, you have turned it into a piece of family history.

The quilts and directions in this book are here to inspire you to design your own family keepsake quilt. The chapter on memory quilts may jog your own memories and give you ideas for making a quilt honoring a favorite place, person, or event in your life. Patterns are given for easy-to-make quilts for special people and occasions. Several ways of printing photos on fabric are discussed in detail so that you can determine which method is best for the type of quilt you are making. There is also information on making a special quilt label with your signature and other pertinent information.

Family keepsake quilts of the past

The history of quilts made for special family events may be as long as the history of quilt-making itself. There are antique quilts made to celebrate a wedding or the birth of a child. There are family genealogy quilts in which 19th-century quilters embroidered family records onto quilt blocks. There are album quilts made by families and friends and given to young pioneer wives to ease their journeys west.

The earliest known bed quilt that contains family genealogical information was part of the DAR Museum's Family Record Exhibit shown in Washington, D.C., in 1989. The medallion-style quilt top was made by Ann Taylor in 1798, soon after her husband was lost at sea. The center portion of the quilt includes the Taylor's marriage date and the birth and death dates of their children. Like so many quilters after her, Ann used her needle skills to record details of her family life.

Early examples of family heritage quilts have been uncovered in many of the state quilt projects in the last decade. A charming quilt documented by the California Heritage Quilt Project is The Albert Quilt. It was made in Pennsylvania in 1917 by Harriet Newel Hurd Thomas for her

great-grandson's fourth birthday. The dates on the quilt refer to the year of Harriet's birth and the year the quilt was made.

"The Albert Quilt," 29½" x 41½", made in 1917 by Harriet Newel Hurd Thomas (1829-1927). Collection of Mr. and Mrs. J.A. Thomas, Jr. Photo by Sharon Risedorph, courtesy of the California Heritage Quilt Project.

The contemporary quilts in this book were made for the same reasons that these and many other antique quilts were made–to honor familial relationships, to celebrate a family event, and to give solace in times of turmoil or grief. By examining how other quilters have chosen to stitch their legacies, perhaps you will be inspired to design your own family heirloom.

Like quiltmakers of the past, we want to leave a legacy that says, "I was here and I cared about my family." A treasured family keepsake quilt is a way of doing that. As our families become increasingly scattered, these quilts become important bonds between generations and between family members who may seldom see one another. These quilts are one way quiltmakers have of keeping families tied together with bits of cloth and love.

Family Genealogical Quilts

In the 19th century there was a great surge of interest in family genealogy. Elaborate family records were penned in the family Bible, professional artists were commissioned to paint decorative framed panels listing family members, and young girls embroidered their family records on needlework samplers.

In the United States in the past 20 years, interest has increased in seeking out family roots. People are searching through county records, interviewing elderly family members in an effort to capture early memories, and looking at old family records and photographs to piece together their family lines. A quilt that incorporates such information about your family is one way of making a record that will be cherished by future generations.

A family genealogical quilt can take many forms. It may be as simple as embroidering or writing family names on pieced blocks. A family tree quilt may include names of family members long gone. It might take the form of an appliquéd tree with each family member's name on a leaf of the tree, or each family branch might be represented by a house on the quilt. The quilts shown here can help you design your own genealogical quilt.

When planning a family quilt, ask yourself these questions concerning what you want to include on it. By focusing on the names you want to include, you will get an idea of the size of the project and you can then choose an appropriate design.

▲ Will the quilt be your family tree (your siblings, parents, grandparents), or your children's tree that would include your spouse's relatives as well?

▲ Will it include all branches or follow one family line only? For instance, you might choose to include only the maternal or paternal side of

"Friendship Wheel," 80" x 80", made in 1915, probably to mark a marriage or anniversary. Photograph courtesy of Thos. K. Woodard American Antiques & Quilts.

your family. The family genealogy quilt shown on page 14 uses pieced houses to document both my husband's and my own immediate families, while the one shown at the top of page 15 documents only one branch of my mother-in-law's family.

▲ Will the quilt be a record of your present family? Or will it include your ancestral family as well?

▲ If you want to include ancestors, how many previous generations will be included? At this point, you may realize that incorporating several past generations may be too difficult, especially if names of family ancestors cannot be retrieved. And it is possible that one branch of your family has been well-documented and another branch is very sketchy and may include little information.

Once you have decided how many generations and what branches of the family to include, there are other questions:

▲ Do you want to include birth dates of all members? Dates of death?

▲ Will you indicate on the quilt where family members live(d)? Any mention about countries of origin?

▲ Will you include everyone's last name? Maiden names? Middle names?

▲ How will you show relationships between generations so the quilt can be informative to others?

▲ Will you include names of all in-laws? Divorced in-laws? Stepchildren?

▲ How will you incorporate informa-

tion about the making of the quilt—a vital piece of information on any quilt you hope to hand down in your family? It should include the maker(s), the occasion for the quilt, where and when it was made, and any other information you feel is relevant. See the chapter on special labels.

Once you have answered these questions, you can begin planning the design that will incorporate your family names. The quilts in this chapter should give you some ideas.

Connie Strech Nordstrom of Cedar Hill, New Mexico, designed and made a delightful quilt using machine appliqués to represent the Wagoner Family Tree (shown below). Each block includes details that give clues to the identity, residence, and interests of each family member. The top row of blocks shows a church with the name of the town where her parents were married and a barn inked with her mother's maiden name. In the second row, the left block represents Connie and her husband. Her parents are the couple holding hands. Her brother's name is in the block with the pickup truck and surfboard. The third-row blocks include one representing her daughter and son-in-law, her nephew, and her niece. The bottom-row blocks represent a second daughter and Connie's son. Married family members have a house in their blocks and single children are shown as people without houses. Patterns for some of the images shown on Connie's quilt are given on pages 52-53 so

"Wagoner Family Tree," 46½" x 45", made by Connie Nordstrom for her parents. Patterns for making a similar quilt are on pages 52 and 53.

that you can make a similar family tree quilt.

When we think of family genealogy, an image of trees comes to mind. Trees were often painted or embroidered as part of elaborate family records made in the 19th century. An appliquéd or pieced tree allows you to place many names on the quilt in nearly any position. This type of design works well if there are several branches of one family and if no more than three or four generations are included. Names can be embroidered or written on the branches and leaves and on fruit or small hearts hanging from the tree.

The quilt shown below is a four-generation tree with tracings of 81 family members' hands. It was made by Maryloo Roberts Stephens of Ogden, Utah, and quilted by Maryloo, Janet Roberts Blamforth, and other relatives and friends for the 60th wedding anniversary of Maryloo's parents in 1978. The parents' names and wedding date are embroidered on the base of the tree. Their children and children's spouses are represented by the darkest blue hand prints closest to the

"Many Hands Quilt," 83" x 83", made by Maryloo R. Stephens and relatives for a 60th wedding anniversary. Photograph by Ronald Read, courtesy of the Church of Jesus Christ of Latter-Day Saints Museum of Church History and Art.

trunk. The medium blue hand prints are of grand-children, and the lightest blue are great-grandchildren. The numbers on the hands represent the birth order within the family, and the unnumbered hand prints represent in-laws. The youngest child represented was only three days old when the hand print was taken. This design works well for this family because there are several family branches and each branch is relatively full.

For a family that does not have as many branches, or for one in which some branches contain many names and other branches contain few members, a tree with appliquéd leaves would be more workable. To make the design symmetrical,

additional leaves (with no embroidered names) can be added where needed.

Another type of family tree quilt includes a block for each family member represented (shown below). When the four daughters of Manley and Millie McGregor of South Haven, Kansas, decided to make a quilt for their parents' 50th wedding anniversary, they enlisted my help in the design. An appliquéd peach-colored heart is cross stitched with each grandchild's name and birth date. The names of the four daughters and sons-in-law and their wedding dates are cross stitched on the green hearts. The couple's wedding portrait, developed on fabric with Kwik

"Manley and Millie's Anniversary Quilt," 70" x 70", made by Judy Hill, Dianne Gile, Nancy Quillin, Paula Sterns, and Vivian Ritter for a 50th wedding anniversary. The photograph was made with Kwik Print™ following the directions given in the chapter about photographs on fabric .

"Family Tree," 70" x 70", made by Theresa Eisinger with the help of relatives for a 40th wedding anniversary.

Print™ (see page 28), is in the upper left corner. The central block is a cross-stitched farm scene surrounded by images from the couple's life together—their church involvement, love of music, his World War II service, and her nursing career. The borders contain stenciled wheat shocks symbolic of his years as a farmer.

The daughters—Judy Hill, Dianne Gile, Nancy Quillin, and Paula Sterns—each contributed her own special needlework skills to make the quilt a one-of-a-kind record of love for their parents. To allow every family member to contribute to the quilt, messages to the anniversary couple were written on a 30" square of muslin, then this

"love letter" was stitched to the back of the quilt. A photo of that label is on page 41.

Many traditional pieced blocks have names that may hold special meaning for a family member. When Theresa Eisinger of Wheatridge, Colorado, joined with other family members Mary Coon, Donna Hamm, and Peggy Spradlin to make a 40th wedding anniversary quilt for their parents, Walter P. and Dorothy J. Thummel, they chose a traditional block with a name that related appropriately to each of the 11 Thummel children. (The quilt is shown above.) Moving clockwise from the Wedding Ring block (top row, second from left), the blocks are Florida Star, Farmer's

"Family Heritage," 58" x 58", made by the author. The photographs are cyanotype sun prints, described in the chapter on photographs on fabric. Patterns for the house and tree blocks are on pages 55-56.

Fields, Red Cross, Ohio Star, Nebraska Windmill, Farmer's Wife, Goldenrod, Lincoln, Colorado Beauty, Sunflower variation, and Cornhusker Star. Each block is embroidered with the child's name and birth date. Hundreds of traditional blocks have names that could apply to your family members. Looking through a book of traditional patterns will soon spark your imagination. *(See the source list at the back of the book.)*

A genealogical quilt that is made with pieced houses for each family allows a great deal of flexibility in design. The quilt can be made square, horizontal, or vertical, depending on the number of family branches to be shown and how they are related. Three examples are shown here.

The first example (above) is a five-generation family tree of my children. Their great-grandparents' photos on fabric are in the top row; their grandparents are in the next row down. (See the

chapter on photographs on fabric for instructions for this process.) Their aunt, uncles, and parents have houses with the names of their children on the windows. Then those same children have their own houses immediately under each parent. Finally, names of *their* children are on the windows. Pieced trees are included as "fillers" to make the quilt symmetrical, and a poem and information about the making of the quilt are cross stitched on two blocks on the bottom row.

The vertical quilt shown opposite is a four-generation family tree of Cora Ritter, my mother-in-law. Her parents, Floyd and Viola McGregor, are represented by a house at the top of the quilt. A cross-stitched poem written by Viola is to the right of the house, and information about the couple is on the left. Their countries of origin—Scotland and Germany—are named on pieced blocks in the corners.

14

The five rust-colored houses represent my mother- and father-in-law, her siblings, and their spouses. Beneath each of these houses are the houses of the children and their spouses. The grandchildren's names are embroidered on windows of these houses. Pieced blocks are used as fillers where needed for balance.

The horizontal quilt shown below shows the parents, siblings, and all the nieces, nephews, and great-nieces and nephews in my mother's and father's families. Because of the large number of family members, I included names of my cousins and their children on their parents' houses, but did not include the names of in-laws.

The left half of the quilt represents members of my mother's family, the Hughes; the right half represents my father's side, the Howells. The pieced trees down the middle of the quilt separate my mother's family from my father's. Another way to separate the two families is with color. The houses on the left are rust/brown with blue roofs, and the colors are reversed on the right half. Trees are used to fill in spaces, since my dad's family is smaller and requires fewer houses. Embroidery in the top and bottom borders gives information about the making of the quilt.

These three quilts point out that it is possible to design a genealogical quilt that includes several family branches and generations, or one that is more limited in scope using the same design elements. You may choose to omit in-laws' names because of lack of space. Full names or just

Above, "The Clan," 30" x 45", made by the author. The patterns for the house and pieced message blocks are on pages 55-57. Below, "Hughes/Howell Family Tree Quilt," 60" x 34", made by the author. This is a five-generations family tree. Patterns are on pages 55-56.

first names may be used. Color coordinating embroidered or inked names makes family relationships clearer.

On page 54 are small blocks that can be used to design your own family house quilt. Full-size patterns for the house, tree, and message blocks are given on pages 55-57.

There are several ways that you can make the family relationships on a genealogical quilt clearly understood. Color can be used to identify various generations, just as Maryloo did with the hand prints on her quilt on page 11, and as I did with the house quilts. All the names of one family branch could be embroidered in the same color, with each branch a different color. Embroidered symbols such as hearts or stars might be used to identify close relationships. Birth order could be designated with numbers before each name. A deceased family member might have an appropriate symbol by his or her name.

Generations, shown above, a quilt that is quite different from the previous examples, was made by Carol Boyer of Syracuse, New York. It honors six generations of women in her family. She chose to follow a strictly maternal path in depicting her family line. Her quilt includes appliquéd articles owned by the various women, including baby dresses, a lace collar, handkerchief, gloves, eyeglasses, and even an infant's hospital bracelet.

The embroidered writing on the quilt reads like the entries in a family Bible. Note that each woman is the first born of her generation. "Sophia Winklman Kellenbarger, born Sept. 12, 1837, in Switzerland. This first child married a German George Kellenbarger and settled in Iowa. She died in 1888. Their first child was Margaret Kellenbarger Gast. Born Feb. 18, 1873, she died 1955. Her and Tarrogut Gast's first child was Ruth Mary Gast Cocklin, born Nov. 18, 1898, married Howard Cocklin, in the Little Brown Church in the Vale. Margaret Marie Cocklin McElhinney was born June 6, 1924. This oldest child married the oldest son, one James Howard McElhinney, on Christmas Eve. Carol Kay McElhinney Boyer born Saturday April 24, 1948, in Keokuk, Iowa. Carol, the first child, married Eric Russel Boyer, also the oldest child. Their first child was Wendy Kay Boyer, born November 19, 1969, at 1:27 A.M. in Marion, Indiana."

Carol's quilt is not only a record of the maternal line in her family—it also is a way of making those women's lives seem more real because of the articles she chose to place on the quilt. And one of the reasons that we make family quilts is to connect present-day generations with those that have passed and the ones yet to come.

"Generations," 42" x 66", made by Carol Boyer to represent six generations of women in her family.

Memory Quilts

We all have special memories of people, places, and events. As those memories begin to fade, a quilt that helps us hold on to those images of remembered places and favorite times will be a treasure. The quilt can be as simple as a scrap quilt made from fabrics that help us remember a loved one to a more elaborate sampler with appliquéd scenes from the past.

When Lucile Weisbrod's daughter was first born, Lucile knew that someday she would make a quilt for her, and she wanted that quilt to be as sentimental as the quilts made for her when she was a child. So Lucile began saving fabric from her daughter Lorann's clothes. Finally,

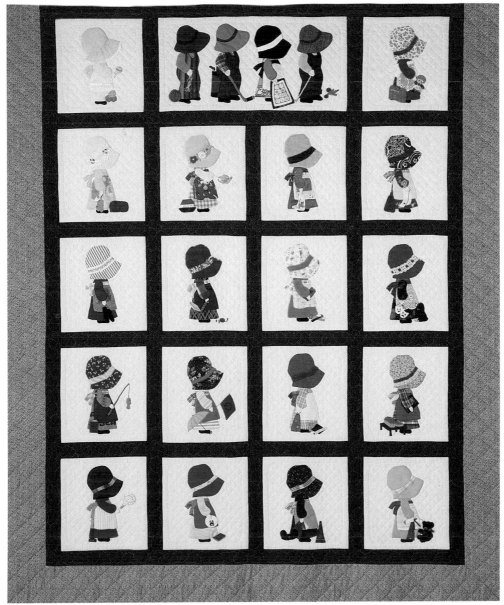

"Lorann's Quilt," 80" x 84", made by Lucile Weisbrod for her daughter's high school graduation.

Lucile fashioned the fabric bits and pieces into a delightful high school graduation quilt.

In the quilt she made, each of the 18 appliquéd sunbonnet girls represents a year in Lorann's life in Rochester, Minnesota. The clothing on each figure is made from garments Lorann wore during that year, and other appliquéd details represent her interests and events during those years. For example, there is a favorite doll at age two, drama masks for the time she was in a play, and mouseketeer ears to recall their vacation at Disneyland. The four Sunbonnet and Overall Sam figures at the center top depict other Weisbrod family members.

Barbara Barber of Westerly, Rhode Island, also used scraps from chil-

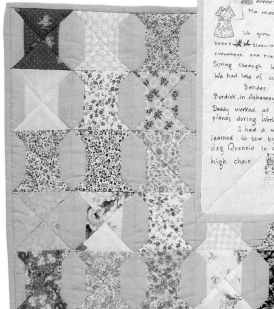

dren's clothing to make memory quilts. She made a Spools quilt for each of her granddaughters using scraps she found in her mother's attic that were leftovers from her own childhood. Barbara wanted to share a bit of her growing up with her granddaughters, so she wrote an illustrated story on the back of the quilt. She wrote about selling vegetables with her father from the back of their truck and about her mother sewing pretty dresses. Barbara remembered sewing clothes for her dog Queenie and placing the dog in a doll's high chair. Her words are interspersed with drawings and appliqué.

Your memory quilt could be made from scraps of a child's clothing, and the story on the back could be about that child's early years.

Left and above, "Spools," 15" x 15", and back label, made by Barbara W. Barber.

Below, "Three Daughters," 25" x 22", by Mary Beth Church.

(What child doesn't like to hear what he was like as a baby?) Include funny incidents you remember, something humorous the child said at an early age, perhaps the first airplane ride, or favorite pets or bedtime songs. The more personal and specific you can make it, the more fun it will be for the child to read.

Portraits in appliqué

Often we honor a person by stitching his or her portrait in cloth. Mary Beth Church of Littleton, Colorado, made a portrait in cloth of her three daughters reading a book (below). The photograph of the scene on the next page can be compared to the wall quilt. The simplicity of her design demonstrates that only the basic details need to be included to make the portrait interesting. Mary Beth used the enlarged tracing to make her appliqué templates.

If you want to stitch a person's portrait, here are a few guidelines to help you in choosing a photograph to interpret in cloth.

▲ The person(s) in the photograph

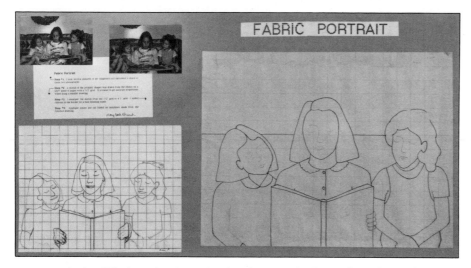

FABRIC PORTRAIT

A simplified tracing is made of a photograph, then enlarged to make appliqué templates.

should be involved in an activity. A posed studio portrait that focuses on the face will be harder to interpret in cloth. But if the subject is throwing a football, the clothing and activity will identify the person, and you don't have to be so concerned about "getting the face right."

▲ The sharper the photograph and the more contrast between subject and background, the easier it will be for you to trace.

▲ Do not eliminate an otherwise good photograph because the background is too busy or there is something extraneous in the scene. Remember that you are *interpreting* the photograph, not making an exact duplicate of it. You can eliminate whatever you don't want in your appliqué or move things around.

Once you have chosen the photograph to interpret in cloth, follow these steps:

1 Place a piece of tracing paper over the photograph. Trace the outline of the figure(s) and objects you want to include. Simplify the lines for appliqué, adding just enough detail so the objects

Original photograph.

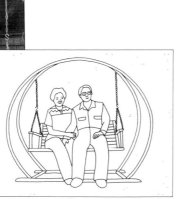

Simplified tracing.

are recognizable. Don't mark every line and shadow on the face. Think of this portrait more as a caricature.

2 Have the tracing enlarged on a copy machine to the desired finished size.

3 When interpreting the portrait in cloth, simplify the pattern even more if necessary for ease in stitching. Use embroidery for details.

Freezer paper appliqué

Details of an appliquéd photograph may be represented by shapes smaller than you are used to stitching. There are several methods of preparing patches for appliqué, including this technique of using freezer paper to make it easier to stitch small shapes.

1 Remove some of the "stick" from the freezer paper by ironing a paper towel onto the shiny side. Pull off the paper towel. (If you skip this step, the paper will be more difficult to remove from the appliqué patches later.)

2 Place the piece of freezer paper shiny side down on top of the drawn design. Trace the patch with no turn-under allowances added. Cut the freezer paper pattern on the drawn line.

Trace shape on freezer paper and cut out.

3 Place the resulting paper pattern shiny side up on the wrong side of the fabric. Cut around the pattern, leaving a scant ³⁄₁₆" turn-under allowance, less if it is a very small patch. Clip into inside curves and corners.

4 With the tip of a warm, dry iron, press the fabric turn-under allowance onto the paper until the fabric sticks in place. Work to make as smooth a turn as possible.

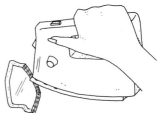

Press fabric seam allowance over edge of freezer paper.

Do not turn under edges that will be positioned beneath other patches.

5 If any of the freezer paper is still exposed, the patch can be positioned on the background fabric simply by pressing it in place with the warm iron. Or pin or baste the patch in place.

6 Begin blindstitching the patch. Before finishing stitching, use tweezers to remove the freezer paper pattern. If necessary, place a warm iron on the patch briefly and the paper will be released more easily. *Or* stitch the patch completely, then cut a small slit on the back side of the background fabric beneath the patch and remove the freezer paper with tweezers. If it is a small patch and difficult to remove the freezer paper, I often leave the paper in place. These appliquéd portraits are not likely to be washed, and the paper would not be a problem if they were ever washed.

Remove freezer paper from appliquéd patch.

"Grampa Howell's Farm," 25" x 30", by the author.

Appliquéd places

We all have special places that we love to visit, if only in our memories. Many quiltmakers have stitched portraits of their homes, vacation spots they have visited, and other places they hold dear.

The 100-year-old log cabin that Cindy Vermillion-Davis and her husband purchased became the living room of the larger house they built in Pagosa Springs, Colorado. Cindy's quilt, The Golden Years (left), captures in cloth not only the house, but her pets–including the peacock that sleeps on her roof. Her three children are represented by the three gold stars.

My childhood summers always included time spent on my Grampa Howell's farm in southeastern Oklahoma. When I made a quilt (above) to remember those times, I chose the events that seemed most important to me at that age. Of course, a quilt of the same place and time made by an older cousin might have different images, but for me, my memory quilt had to include the ball game Annie Over, a cousin sliding down the barn roof, a giant tarantula that crept into the yard, the fish we tried to catch but never could, and my grandmother in her bonnet working in her carefully tended garden.

"The Golden Years," 46" x 53", made by Cindy V. Davis as a memory quilt of her and her husband's country home.

20

Your memory of a place can be the only significant source you have to create the images for your quilt. The scenes don't need to be exactly correct in every detail. Leave out what is not important, change the perspective of the buildings if that makes a better picture, place seasonal things in the picture even if they could not all be there at the same time. Change proportion, perhaps enlarging some of those images that seem to have made the greatest impressions. Alter colors and juxtapositions. Try to create the mood, the feeling that the place gives. For example, when I designed "Grampa Howell's Farm," I did not have a picture of the barn, so I designed a generic barn. I made the stream more important than it probably was in relation to the entire scene. I included only those buildings and images that have significance for me.

However, if you want to make a quilt that is a more exact portrait of a place, then you can work from photographs. Gather the photos you plan to use. It's likely that if your quilt is a scene

Four photographs used for appliquéd block.

with several images, you will have to use more than one picture, and they will probably not all be in the same perspective or scale. Here are guidelines to consider when designing a memory quilt from photographs.

1 Place a piece of tracing paper over the photograph and trace the main lines of the scene. Simplify each part by eliminating unnecessary lines and shadows on the photograph. Trace

the background lines, including the horizon if it shows. The most important parts of a building to include are the roof line, the windows and doors, and any other main identifying features. Remember that you are interpreting these images in cloth, and you only need enough of the shape to indicate what they are.

Top, original photo; bottom, simplified tracing. Note that this figure was flopped for the scene shown below.

Feel free to change the lines of any part to make the shapes easier to appliqué, or change the perspective or proportion. Note that the road in the photograph at far left was shifted in the final scene shown below. If you are working from more than one photograph, trace only the portions of each that you plan to include.

2 Have the tracings enlarged or reduced on a copy machine to the desired finished size.

3 Once you have each part the correct size, tape them in place on a sheet of paper, or trace over the shapes on tracing paper to make the overall design. (See the finished scene on the bottom row of the quilt on the back cover.)

4 When stitching the scene, use printed fabrics to simplify the appliqué. Rather than stitching all the crags and crannies of a mountain peak, use a print that will give the appearance of the mountain's rockiness. See the quilt on the back cover for several examples of scenes that use fabrics in this manner.

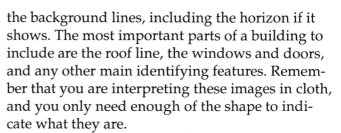

The tracings of the four photographs were enlarged or reduced as needed, then taped together to make the entire scene.

that Caroline planted in their rock garden in front of the house.

Because each block functions like a photograph in an album, she did not need to be concerned about keeping objects in proportion; the water flowers that grow in the lake can be as large as the house when using this design technique.

The house block was drawn from a photograph. First, a small grid was placed over the picture. A piece of paper the size of the quilt block was then marked with an inch-wide grid. Major lines of the house were drawn on the paper, corresponding to the grid lines imposed on the photograph.

Many of the blocks incorporate embroidery for their detail; the water flowers and the grape hyacinths are clusters of french knots, thin stems of poppies are outline stitching, the pine needles are long stitches of beeswaxed green floss, and the small details of the mallard duck are satin stitched.

Above, "Pine Hill Farm," 46" x 46", made by Chris Wolf Edmonds.
Right, "Thorn Lake Album," 45" x 53", made by Caroline Reardon.

Chris Wolf Edmonds lives on Pine Hill Farm near Lawrence, Kansas. Her hanging (above) is a folk-art stylization of her mind's-eye picture of her home, along with her family members and Josh the dog at the lower right. The border is a pieced Pine Tree pattern, to represent the thousands of trees that the Edmondses have planted over the years to sell before Christmas. There are quilted clouds, fields, and trees that accent the appliqué work.

When Caroline Reardon realized that her two daughters were growing up and would soon leave home, she decided to capture in cloth memories of their family life at home near Black Hawk, Colorado. Thorn Lake Album is a sampler quilt showing scenes including the wood pile, their Ashley stove, bread baking, family members biking along the lake shore, the sauna, and the wild flowers

Photographs on Fabric

A photographic image on cloth that is sewn into a quilt top or that is part of a label on the back makes that quilt a personal one and even more of a treasured heirloom. Women have been placing photographs on their quilts for more than a hundred years. I have a Crazy Quilt made early in this century that includes the printed photo of an infant on one of the patches.

Photograph on fabric on a circa-1910 Crazy Quilt patch.

In every workshop I have ever given on family keepsake quilts, one subject that always interests everyone is how to print photos on fabric. We are lucky today to have several techniques that were not available to early quiltmakers. There are directions for several methods in this chapter; each one has its own advantages and disadvantages. Your choices can be made based on the type of image you want on your quilt and the amount of time, money, and effort you wish to spend. With some practice and experimentation, you too can add family photos to your quilts.

For my children's family tree quilt (page 14) with photographs of their grandparents and great-grandparents, I chose the antique look of cyanotype. But on the anniversary quilt made for an aunt and uncle in which all the fabrics were green and peach (page 12), Kwik Print™ was the preferred method since it allowed the photograph to be printed in peach. And on my sister's birthday quilt containing multiple photos (page 30), I used color-copy heat-transfer photographs. Instructions are included for all these methods so you can find one here that meets your needs.

Cyanotype (sun print)

This method of transferring photographs to fabric gives a softly tinted blue-on-white photograph for an old-fashioned look. The technique has been used since the mid-1800s when it was invented for making blueprints on paper. It is as simple as one-two-three. (See the samples on page 25.)

1 White 100%-cotton fabric is treated with chemicals and allowed to dry.

2 Then a negative of the photograph is placed directly on the fabric, covered with glass, and exposed to the sun.

3 The image is developed on the cloth by the sun's light.

The chemicals required can be purchased from a chemical-supply house or specialty company. Or you can order the pretreated fabric and eliminate the step of preparing the cotton yourself. *(See the source list at the end of this book.)*

Advantages of sun printing
▲ looks old-fashioned, good when using photos of ancestors
▲ image is permanent, will not wash out
▲ is printed on 100% cotton, the preferred fabric for quilters
▲ print can be washed, so can be used in bed quilts (Caution: Wash only in mild soap. DO NOT use a phosphate detergent.)
▲ generally gives a detailed print
▲ the negative can be altered to improve the printed image

▲ exposed by sunlight, a source available to everyone at no cost

▲ the negative can be flopped for printing, so you can get a reversed image if desired

Disadvantages of sun printing

▲ purchase of half-tone negatives is required for each photograph to be printed

▲ if coating your own fabric, working with chemicals requires some caution

▲ if coating your own fabric, requires a dark room with a red or yellow safelight (available for about $5 in photo-supply stores)

Preparing the fabric yourself

If you choose to prepare your own fabric, you will need the following:

▲ a dark room (a space with no windows, or a space in which light can be sealed out)

▲ red or yellow safelight

▲ a plastic cloth on a work surface

▲ washed and pressed 100% white cotton fabric cut larger than your negative

▲ sponge craft brush

▲ potassium ferricyanide (handle with care)

▲ ferric ammonium citrate

▲ rubber gloves

1 Work in a dark room with a safelight, and wear gloves and old clothes. Use measuring spoons not used for cooking. Measure and dissolve 1½ teaspoons potassium ferricyanide in ½ cup water in a disposable cup. In another cup, dissolve 1 tablespoon ferric ammonium citrate in ½ cup water. Mix the two solutions together.

2 Lay a fabric square on the covered table. **Warning: Do not splash the chemicals on any surface for they will develop when the light is turned on and are virtually impossible to remove.** Using the sponge brush, paint the chemicals on the fabric, first one direction, then the other. Fabric will be soaked. Repeat for other fabric squares. Coat small 2" squares of fabric that will be used to test printing times.

3 With newspapers underneath to catch drips, suspend the fabric with clothespins on wire hangers or clothesline and dry completely in the dark room. This will take several hours. An electric fan in the room will speed the drying process.

You may want to paint the fabric one night and print the next day. When dry, the fabric will be a light chartreuse green. You can press the cloth with a dry iron if it is wrinkled; do not get it wet once it is dry. Keep the dried fabric in a light-tight box or dark room until printed. It will be usable for several days with no loss of effectiveness as long as light does not strike it.

The negative

The negative, and therefore your sun print, can be no better than your original photograph. Use sharp photographs with good contrast. If there is little contrast between the person in the photograph and the background, then the outline of the person may disappear. You need a negative that is the exact size of the finished print and one that has good contrast between the lights and darks. Here's how to get the negative. Go to a photography shop or look in the yellow pages for lithographers. (*See the source list at the end of the book.*) Provide the shop with your black-and-white or color photograph. Ask for a **half-tone negative** made with 85 to 100 dots per inch. This type of negative has the good contrast necessary to capture details in the faces you print. The shop can enlarge or reduce your photograph to the size negative you need. Remember that your negative must be the same size as you want the photograph to be printed on fabric. Your picture will be returned to you unharmed. The cost of this type of negative is just a few dollars

You may be able to tape several photographs on one sheet of paper. Then one large negative can be made that can be cut apart before printing on fabric. This is called a "gang" negative. Ask your shop about this. (Do not put very dark photos and very light photos on the same sheet.) The negatives can be used over and over without harm to them.

"Gang" negative

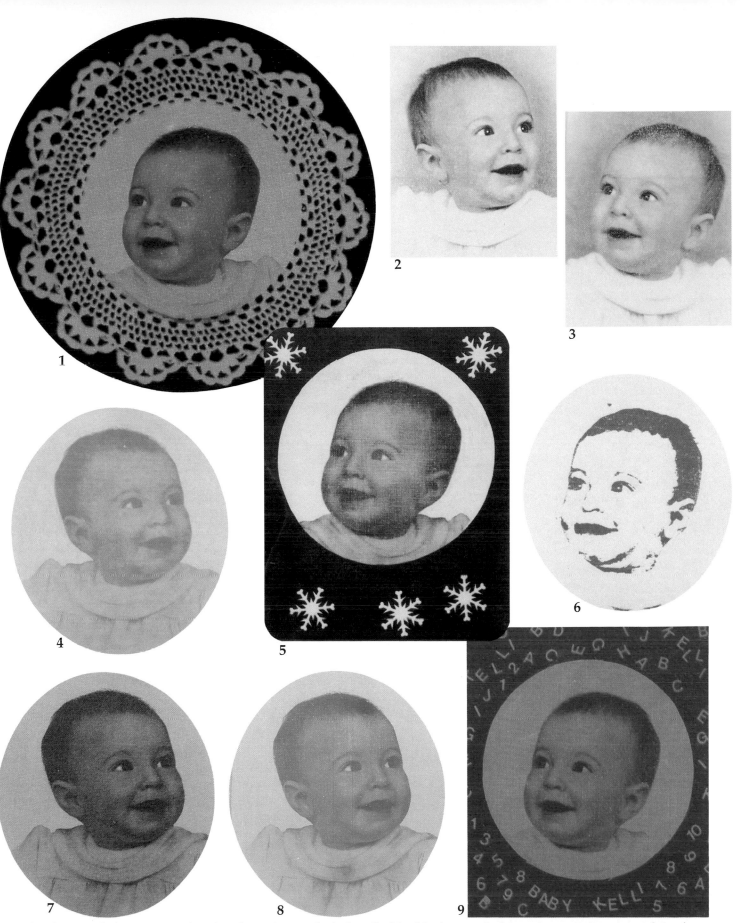

The photographs here were made using the various methods described in this chapter. 1. A two-step cyanotype sun print using a doily as a frame. 2. Color-copy heat transfer. 3. A regular color copy transferred with Picture This™. 4. Inkodye™ sun print. 5. A two-step sun print made with black Kwik Print™; foil snowflakes placed for the second printing. 6. A photo silk screen printed with textile paint. 7. A tea-dyed cyanotype sun print. 8. Green Kwik Print. 9. A two-step cyanotype sun print using press-type letters on clear plastic for the second printing.

Sun printing the fabric

The steps given here are for sun printing a photograph. If you would like to experiment with printing other objects, see pages 33-35.

Whether you purchase pretreated fabric or treat your own as described on page 24, you need the following for printing:

- ▲ half-tone negative for each photograph to be printed
- ▲ clipboard or other board larger than the fabric for moving print outdoors
- ▲ foam rubber as large as the fabric or several layers of paper towels
- ▲ sheet of clean, dry glass larger than the negative
- ▲ timer or watch

Once the fabric is dry (if it feels cool it is still damp), you can begin the printing process. Choose a clear, sunny day. The best time for printing is when the sun is most directly overhead. You can print in the winter, but it will take longer, and the cloth prints may not be as dark or sharp as those printed in the summer. Follow these steps using your small test squares first. Then repeat the process with your larger pieces of fabric.

1 Layer in this order the board, foam rubber, treated fabric, and negative, then the clean, dry glass. The negative can be flopped if desired to give an image that is reversed from the original photograph. Make certain there are no threads on

glass

negative

treated cloth

foam

board

Materials layered for sun printing.

the cloth, for they will leave white squiggles on the print. If there is moisture on the glass, it may distort the image. The glass should be tight enough to flatten the negative and cloth. If necessary, press down and tape the glass to the board. If the negative is not in direct contact with the cloth, the sun will leak in at the edges and the print will be fuzzy.

2 Take this "sandwich" outside and lay it flat on a table or prop it up so that it faces the sun more directly. Do not shift the negative on the cloth. Begin timing. The length of printing time varies with the brightness of the sun. Begin by printing for about 8 to 10 minutes.

3 When the cloth turns a silvery gray, take it inside and rinse the print under cool running water to wash out the chemicals. Pat with paper towels, then air dry. Press with a warm iron if needed. The image turns a darker blue as it dries, and the light details become more distinct.

Tips for improving the sun print

If your first attempts at making a sun print are a bit disappointing, try another. With some practice and experimentation with different exposure times, you may be able to obtain a more satisfactory print.

If the image washes out and there is very little blue, you need a longer exposure time, or you did not allow the fabric to completely dry. If the image is dark blue and there is very little detail, expose for a shorter time.

If you followed the directions carefully and still did not obtain a good sun print, the problem may be that your negative does not have enough contrast. There are a couple of things you can do to alter the negative. Remember that you are working with a negative, so whatever shows black on the negative will be light on the fabric print. Whatever is light or clear on the negative will print dark. You have to think in reverse image. Work on the emulsion (dull) side of the negative. It feels a bit rougher than the shiny side.

Adding shadows: If there is too little detail or the too-light subject gets lost in the light background, you can add shadows. First, hold the negative up to the light to see clearly where the negative is very dark and dense. That is where the print may be too light. Remember, think "in reverse." You can then gently remove some of the emulsion from the dull side of the negative by scratching it with a razor blade or pin. The clear film will be exposed so light can penetrate and create a dark line on the photo. For instance, if the subject's eyes have nearly disappeared, scratch off a little to define eyebrows or pupils. You can add lips, shadows on the face or hair, or separate the figure from the background this way. Don't overdo it, though. Once the emulsion is scratched off it

Altering negatives: The original negative, shown above, has little contrast between the head and background, so in the fabric print the head nearly disappears. The stars on the flag are not very bright.

The negative above has been altered by inking out the background behind the head, adding a few lines to the hair, and inking in stars; the fabric print has more contrast.

is difficult to replace.

Adding light: If the fabric print is too dark and details are lost, you can add ink to the negative so that it will print lighter in some places. As before, hold the negative up to a light source. If the subject's face appears all clear, the face will be dark with no detail on the fabric print. Sometimes two people standing side by side merge together and there is no distinction between them. You might draw a fine line to designate a shoulder or arm to separate them. Use permanent india ink or pens made for writing on acetate. These products are available in art- and office-supply stores. On the dull, rough side of the negative add lines or dots of ink where you want more light on the fabric print. Use the point of a straight pin dipped in the ink to get fine lines. Or cut off most of the bristles of a cheap paintbrush and use that. Remember that the inked portions will print light, not dark. If you want the whites of someone's eyes to show up, place a dot of ink at the corners of their eyes. If you make a mistake, you can gently wipe off the ink before it dries.

In the examples shown above, the first print is too dark. The subject and background blend together. The negative was altered as described above. To lighten the background, india ink was brushed onto the background around the

head, so that when printed the subject is clearer. To separate the back of the head from the dark flag, thin lines were drawn on the hair so there would be highlights when printed on fabric. The stars of the flag also were darkened on the negative so that they printed lighter on the fabric.

Store your negatives flat in a box to keep them from getting scratched. Every unwanted scratch will mar the print. Don't let the negatives get wet. They may be used over and over again.

Turning a blue print to brown

If you want an old-fashioned sepia brown print (see photo number 7 on page 25), follow these instructions from Blueprints in Belmont, California. (*See the address in the source list.*) Make a blue sun print. Wash the print in 1 T. phosphate detergent, such as powdered Tide, dissolved in 2 cups hot water. If you are fading many photos, make a fresh detergent solution often. Rinse the fabric thoroughly. All of the blue will wash out and the print will be a pale yellow. Don't panic. Prepare a tea bath by boiling 3 tea bags in 2 cups water; let steep for 5 minutes and remove bags. Soak the print in the tea bath for 30 minutes or less. The details of the print will be restored to a brown color. Rinse. DO NOT ever bleach the print; you will lose the image.

Kwik Print™

Like cyanotype sun printing, this method requires treating fabric with light-sensitive chemicals, placing a photographic negative on the fabric, and exposing it to a light source. The main advantage is that the Kwik Print comes in many colors that can be mixed like paint to obtain a print that will match the color of your fabric. This does not produce a multi-colored photograph. The print will be rose on white, green on white, or whatever. Examples of photographs printed with this method are on pages 12 and 25.

The chemical may be purchased in 15 different colors packaged in squeeze bottles. (*See the source list for a mail-order company.*) Unlike the cyanotype print, several different fabrics can be printed, including 100% cotton, cotton blends, and polyester.

Advantages of Kwik Print
▲ unlimited colors are possible by mixing
▲ no mixing of chemicals; the squirt bottle is easy to use
▲ fabric can be prepared in low-light room
▲ generally gives a detailed print
▲ the negative can be altered to improve the printed image
▲ can expose by sunlight or a 500-watt light bulb, so you don't have to depend on the sun
▲ the negative can be flopped for printing, so you can get a reversed image if desired

Disadvantages of Kwik Print
▲ purchase of half-tone negative required for each photo to be printed
▲ each color and fabric type has its own exposure time, so testing is required
▲ not all fabrics are printed equally well— some experimentation may be necessary

Preparing the fabric
You need the following:
▲ plastic cloth or newspapers
▲ dimly lit room
▲ sponge craft brush
▲ Kwik Print in color(s) desired
▲ cotton fabric or fabric blend
▲ spray starch if using 100% cotton
▲ iron
▲ rubber gloves

▲ glass larger than fabric square
▲ masking tape
▲ foam rubber larger than fabric or several layers of paper towels
▲ clipboard or other board larger than fabric

1 If using cotton, soak the fabric with spray starch; allow to dry, then iron smooth. The

Starching cotton for printing with Kwik Print.

starch will prevent the color from being absorbed completely into the fibers. If you don't first starch the cotton, you cannot rinse out the Kwik Print after exposure. (If using 100% polyester, starching is not necessary.)

2 Tape all edges of the fabric square to the glass, pulling the fabric taut and smooth.

3 Work in a dimly lit room and wear gloves when painting on the Kwik Print. Mix colors by squirting them into a paper cup and mixing with a plastic spoon. For instance, if you want a grayed blue, start with 2 tablespoons of a basic medium blue, then add a drop of black. *The color dries lighter than the color of the wet paint.*

For a photo about 5" x 7", place 2 tablespoons of the Kwik Print in the center of the fabric square. Using the sponge brush, coat the fabric vertically, then horizontally. If you can't

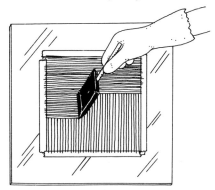

Brushing Kwik Print onto taped fabric.

completely coat the fabric, place a bit more of the chemical where needed. Coat the cloth evenly.

4 Place the fabric (still taped to glass) in a dark room or closet and allow to dry for about one hour. To speed up the process, place an electric fan in the closet. The fabric must be totally dry. If it feels cool, it is still damp.

Printing the fabric

Follow the instructions on page 26 for printing the cyanotype sun print. A half-tone negative is also used in this method. It is possible to print by sunlight or with a 500-watt light bulb in a photoflood lamp positioned one foot above the fabric. The amount of exposure time varies with each color, so testing on small pieces of the fabric will save your chemicals. Begin exposing for five minutes. After exposure, immerse the print in a solution of 1 teaspoon ammonia mixed with one quart water, and then rinse in clear water. If the color washes out and there are no details, next time expose for a longer period. Loss of image could also mean that you did not allow the fabric to dry completely. If the image is dark and shows little detail, expose for a shorter period of time.

Color-copy heat transfer

The methods just described give photographs printed on fabric in one color–blue, brown, or any of the colors of Kwik Print. Color-copy heat transfers on cloth give full-color photographs.

The quilt shown on the following page includes many photos on fabric that were made using this process. The small quilt on the sewing-room wall block shown on the back-cover quilt is also a color-copy heat transfer.

Advantages of the color-copy heat transfer

▲ gives full, fairly bright color
▲ quick and easy, no chemistry involved
▲ no negative is needed
▲ can be printed on 100% cotton fabric
▲ photographs can be enlarged and reduced

Disadvantages of the color-copy heat transfer

▲ copy machine may be difficult to find
▲ image may be reversed

▲ if many photographs are printed, could be costly (about $9–$14 for a sheet 8½" x 11")

Making a color-copy heat transfer

With this method, a photograph is copied onto special heat-transfer paper made for this purpose. Not all copiers handle this special paper. If you can't find a copy store in your area with this capability, you can mail your photographs to one of the places listed in the sources at the end of this book. Or perhaps the T-shirt printing company in your mall will do this for you.

1 If you have a number of photographs you'd like to transfer, tape as many as will fit on an 8½" x 11" piece of typing paper. Also include a small photograph on the paper that you can cut apart and use for testing your iron later.

Photographs ready for printing a color-copy heat transfer.

(If you are sending your photographs to a mail-order company, follow their directions for sending photographs to them. Some require that your photographs be placed no closer than ½" on the sheet of paper to be copied. These companies will send you the photos printed on their cloth.)

2 Take the photographs to your copy store or mail them and ask that they be printed on heat-transfer paper. Once printed, cut apart the copies.

3 To transfer the copy to cloth, set your iron at its highest temperature. Place a piece of your test photograph face down on white fabric. Hold the hot iron in place on the back of the paper copy

"The Photo Gallery," 40" x 48", made by the author for her sister's 50th birthday. The photographs are color-copy heat transfers on cloth. Directions for the Log Cabin blocks are on page 64.

for 30 seconds. Peel off the paper. The photograph will be transferred to the cloth. If your iron is not hot enough, not all of the image will be transferred to the cloth.

Ironing the color-copy heat transfer to fabric.

If you are transferring a large photograph, it will be necessary to iron the copy a portion at a time. Iron one part, then move the iron to the next part of the copy. Continue in this manner until you have covered the entire photocopy. If you find that the copy cools down before you can get the entire surface ironed, peel it up a portion at a time. Or find a T-shirt printing shop that will use their flatiron press to iron your prints to your cloth for a small fee. (Mine charged 50¢ for each photo transferred.)

Tips for color-copy heat transfers

▲ The heat transfer on fabric will be no better than the original photograph. A photograph that is dark with low contrast will not transfer successfully.

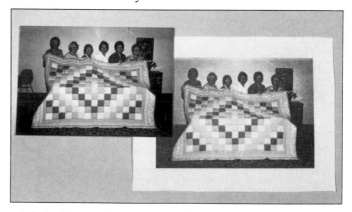

A dark photograph produces a dark color-copy heat transfer.

▲ If you wish to use black-and-white photographs, ask that the color copy machine be turned to black and white. Otherwise, the machine may pick up odd tints of color. Or have the photo printed in one color. Your black-and-white photograph can be printed in all red, or black, or blue, etc. The photographs on Our Family Wedding Quilt shown at right are examples of this one-color heat-transfer method.

▲ Depending on whether the copy machine you use reverses the original photograph or not, when you iron the copy onto fabric, the image may be reversed–not necessarily bad for a photograph of a person, but a house or landscape looks odd in reversed image. Ask the machine operator if the image on the cloth will be like the original. Some mail-order companies print the image so it is the same orientation as the original photograph. If this is important to you, ask the company when writing if the image on cloth is reversed or not. Some machines make copies from slides (enlarged to the desired size). The slide can be turned backwards before copying so the copy will be a reversed image. When ironed on fabric, the image will be in the correct orientation.

▲ These machines also can enlarge and reduce your photographs. This allows you to use small prints as well as larger portraits on the same quilt by having them changed to similar sizes. Just be sure to tell the operator if you wish to have any changed in size. All photographs taped to the same sheet of paper will be reduced or enlarged at the same percentage.

"Our Family Wedding Quilt," 36" x 36", made by Caroline Reardon for her daughter and son-in-law. The portraits on fabric are of the parents and grandparents of the bride and groom. The center portrait is of the wedding couple. The photographs and printed names are color-copy heat transfers.

A large photograph was reduced and a small photograph was enlarged to approximately the same size by the color-copy heat-transfer method.

Other methods

There are still other methods of transferring photos to fabric that you might find interesting to explore. Inkodye™ is yet another light-sensitive chemistry that is painted on the cloth, then exposed to sun. It is very similar to the Kwik Print™ method described earlier, and the product gives an infinite range of colors. The Inkodye is made especially for natural fibers, so it is not necessary to starch the cotton fabric before printing. The fabric can be coated in incandescent light. (It will expose in sunlight and fluorescent light.) The color is pale when it is coated and turns darker with exposure. See photograph number 4 on page 25 for an example.

If you are familiar with silk-screen printing, then you may be interested in a photo silk-screen method. An example is photograph 6 on page 25. The print is less like a photograph than the other methods described–it gives a more graphic image. If you want only one photograph, then this method is time-consuming. But if you want to make multiple copies of the same photograph, then this method should be explored. A child's quilt with multiple images of the child printed in different colors could be a fun project. Hunt Speedball™ makes a product that uses a silk screen and textile paints to obtain photographs on fabric. This method is fully described in the directions that come with the product.

There are several products on the market that are used to obtain a full-color photo on fabric. Picture This™ and Pictures to Fabric™ are two products using this process. This method is similar to making a decal. A liquid medium is brushed onto the image–a magazine print on slick paper or a regular color copy of a photograph.

Rubbing the paper backing from a photocopy that has been treated with Picture This.

The print is adhered to fabric and allowed to dry. It is immersed in water, then the paper backing is rubbed off, leaving the image on the cloth. Complete directions come with each product. Photo 3 on page 25 was made with Picture This, as was the black-and-white photograph on label 1 on page 38.

Another method that gives a bright, glossy, full-color image is Transfer Magic™. It would be suitable for a child's wall quilt that is

Rubbing Transfer Magic onto a regular color copy.

not intended to be washed often. The transfer feels a bit rubbery, and the image is not reversed. Transfer Magic is a clear adhesive plastic that may be available in fabric or craft-supply stores. (*See the source list at the end of the book.*) The cost is about $2 for a sheet 5" x 7". The package of Transfer Magic comes with excellent, detailed instructions. Briefly, the plastic is adhered to a regular color copy of a photograph, the backing is rubbed off, then the image is transferred to cloth. I used this product to copy the small photos and tiny magazine covers in the sewing room block and rocking chair block on the back-cover quilt.

All of the various methods of transferring photographs to fabric leave your original photos intact and unharmed. Therefore, you can use your most precious photos to add those images to your quilted projects.

What could be more personal than a photograph on a quilt? There will be no doubt who the quilt is for if the recipient's photograph is placed either on the front or lining of the quilt. Photographs of ancestors on your family tree quilt will add a touch of history, and future generations will feel more connected to the quilt and to their forebears when these images are part of their quilt heritage.

Having fun
with sun prints

Anything that blocks out the sun can be used to make a sun print–natural objects and found items, crocheted doilies and lace, drawings, stencils–let your imagination soar.

The ideas we offer here can be used with all of the methods described in this chapter that use the sun for printing on fabric. Read through this list, and perhaps you'll think of other objects in your home and surroundings that will personalize your sun prints even more.

▲ Natural objects like grasses, ferns, flowers, and leaves can be placed on the treated fabric to make a print for use in a block or to form a frame around photos. If no glass is used to flatten the object, interesting shadows will be formed by the raised portions. See label 5 on page 38.

▲ Laces, doilies, and anything with an open texture can be printed. If your great-grandmother did crochet or other fancy needlework with open spaces, you could print a piece of her work on the fabric. Place the needlework on the dried treated cloth just like a negative. If glass is placed over it, the image will print sharper. If no glass is used to keep the needlework flat, there will be interesting shadows and softer lines of printing.

▲ Paper cutouts made with black construction paper make frames around photo-

"Mommom's Quilt," 34" x 34", made by Susan Hazel for her grandmother. The photographs and printed names are sun prints. The label above with the recipient's photograph is on the back of the quilt.

graphs. Cut an oval, circle, or square in the center of the paper and place over the photographic negative, allowing the portrait to show in the cutout. The cutouts will prevent the fabric around the photograph from printing, so the picture will be neatly framed with white all around. See photos 4, 6, 7, and 8 on page 25 and the quilt on page 33.

▲ To obtain a photograph that is framed with a doily or other objects like samples 1, 5, and 9 on page 25, you need to sun print the same fabric twice, covering up each time the portion that you don't want printed. First, place the negative on the treated sun-print fabric and place a frame of construction paper with a cutout as described above. Cover with glass and print in the sun. Take

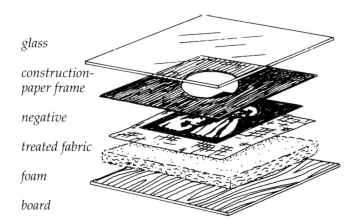

glass

construction-paper frame

negative

treated fabric

foam

board

Two-step sun print.

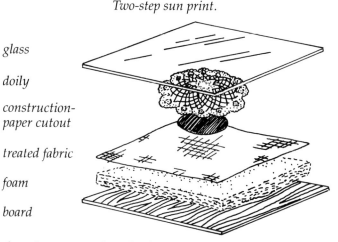

glass

doily

construction-paper cutout

treated fabric

foam

board

the photo "sandwich" back into a dark room and remove the paper frame. Place the circle that was cut from the paper on top of the fabric exactly in the printed circle area. (You will be able to see where it has printed.) Place the doily, natural objects, press-type letters, or whatever you want printed around the photo on top. Return to the sun and print for the full time once again. Rinse and dry the print.

▲ Images drawn or pasted to clear plastic (acetate) will print in a negative image. In other words, whatever is drawn in black on the acetate will print white on a colored background. Use india ink or pens made for writing on acetate. Draw words or pictures on the acetate and use like a negative for printing on the treated cloth. To get the image of a house, place the acetate on top of a photograph of the building and trace over the main lines. You can shade with lines or dots. The printed image will have the lines white with all else printed blue (or whatever color of Kwik Print™ you are using). This negative image may

Drawing on acetate that has been sun printed.

look odd for a portrait of a person, but it is interesting for buildings or other designs.

▲ Press-type letters (the kind used to make posters), available in art- and office-supply stores, can be pressed onto the acetate to write names and messages. When printed, the letters will be white on a colored background. This is one effective method of writing names that does not

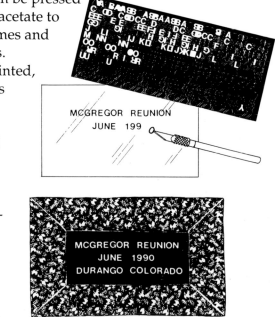

Press-type letters on acetate that have been sun printed.

require embroidery or good penmanship. The press type can also be placed directly onto the treated cloth and printed.

▲ Copy machines can print on acetate provided by the copy store for about 50¢–75¢ per sheet. You can copy photographs of buildings, wedding invitations, and other written material.

Photograph of a house photocopied onto acetate then sun printed.

Ask the copy-machine operator to turn the black-and-white copier to dark. You will get a positive image on the acetate. Sun print with the acetate on treated fabric. What is dark on the acetate will print white on a colored background. See label 3 on page 38.

The blocks on pages 58-59 have been specifically designed to be copied onto acetate and sun printed. The center of each block is left blank for a signature. When printed on fabric the centers will be white. See label 7 on page 38 and the quilt on page 46.

▲ If you want names and words that are dark on a white background, then have a negative made. If you have access to a computer, you can generate many sizes of letters in different fonts (letter styles). Print out all the names/words you need, then have a half-tone or a continuous-line negative made (the photo shop will know what these are), just like the ones for printing photographs on fabric. (*See the source list at the end of the book.*) Cut the negative apart and make a sun print of each portion. The words will be printed in color on a white background. These printed

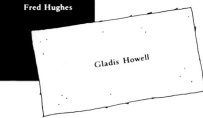

Names were typed on a computer, then a negative was made of the list. The names were cut apart and sun printed.

names could be appliquéd underneath the photographs. Or print the names at the same time you are printing the photos. The names on the quilt shown on page 33 and label 5 on page 38 were printed with this method.

▲ Anything that blocks out the sun can be printed. Look around your house for interesting shapes of jewelry, or kitchen and office supplies. Glitter and other foil shapes can be fun to use. See the snowflakes around photo 5 on page 25. Stencils that will block out the sun make lovely sun prints. If you want a place for writing a signature on the sun print, tape a piece of cardboard where needed to block out the sun before printing.

Stencil taped to fabric, then sun printed. The words are written with permanent-ink pen.

Special Labels

Perhaps the easiest–but most important–thing you can do to make any quilt more of a family keepsake quilt is to sign it. If you plan for your quilts to be passed down from one family member to another, then you surely do not want the quilt's maker to become anonymous. "Who made this quilt? Was it Dad's Grandmother or Mom's?" After all, it is your way of saying "I was here." And any antique dealer or quilt historian will tell you that a signed and dated quilt is more valuable, not only on the quilt market, but to the family members who inherit it.

Here is the information you should consider including on a signature label:

▲ your full name, including your middle name and maiden name if applicable
▲ the full name of the recipient
▲ your relationship to the recipient
▲ where you both live
▲ the date of completing the quilt, or the dates of the start and finish
▲ any significant information about the quilt itself such as the block name or design
▲ the occasion for making the quilt–a wedding, graduation, birth
▲ a message of love, congratulations, or whatever is appropriate to the recipient
▲ a history of the quilt (may be added later), including exhibits where it was displayed
▲ an indication of the quilt's recipients: "To my daughter Sara and in turn to her daughter Kim."
▲ washing/care instructions

Quilted labels

A subtle and elegant way to add information is to stitch it into the quilting design. If the quilt has a border, that is a good place to quilt your name, date, and whatever other information you want to include. Or you might replace one patch within a block with a solid-colored fabric in which you quilt the label. If you wish the quilting to be more noticeable, use contrasting thread as shown in label 9 on page 38.

Embroidered labels

Many styles are possible with embroidery–from a child's name colorfully cross-stitched with yarn in the center of a crib quilt to a delicately scrolled signature finely stitched with one strand of floss.

Threads other than embroidery floss can be used. If it is washable and small enough to be put through a needle's eye, then you can use it for signing. Pearl cotton, regular sewing thread, metallic thread, and baby-weight yarn each will give a distinctive look. You may want to embroider directly on the lining or on a quilt block or border on the quilt front. A separate label stitched to the lining is also an easy and effective way to add information. And a separate label allows you to place the information on those quilts now that you never got around to labeling earlier.

Counted-thread embroidery

Some embroidery stitches such as cross stitch and backstitch are designed to be worked over even-weave cloth to give your labels a distinctive look. The use of this type of background cloth eliminates the need for marking, and the words and names will be neat and even, a plus if you don't want to write free-hand on your label.

Although even-weave cloth such as Aida cloth, hardanger, or linen is thicker than the fabrics used for piecing, it can be substituted for cotton in patches. (The larger the patch, the easier it is to handle the Aida cloth.) Even-weave cloth is available in quilt and needlework shops in sizes 6 to 32 or more threads per inch. The more squares per inch, the smaller your stitches will be. The examples shown opposite illustrate the difference between three sizes of even-weave cloth. The same alphabet is used on the three samples.

26 threads per inch.

16 threads per inch.

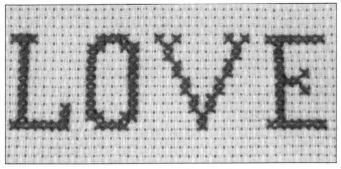

11 threads per inch. These samples are shown actual size.

Using even-weave cloth

1 Choose the alphabet you want to use. For long messages, it is best to use a small-size alphabet, with the lower-case letters 3 to 7 stitches high. Many books with plain and fancy alphabets for cross stitching and backstitching are available. Because backstitched letters are often stitched over fewer squares of the fabric than cross-

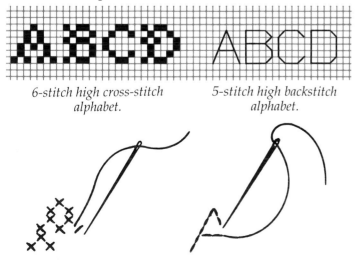

6-stitch high cross-stitch
alphabet.   *5-stitch high backstitch*
                              alphabet.

Each square of the graph equals one square of the
even-weave cloth.

stitched alphabets, they may be better for labels that require many names or words. The labels underneath each block of the quilt on the back cover are made with backstitched letters.

2 Write your message on graph paper using the chosen alphabet, with one square of graph paper equaling one square or thread of the even-weave cloth. If you want all the lines aligned on the left, then write it that way on the graph paper, leaving the desired number of spaces between words and lines. Fold the paper in half to find the center of the longest line. If you want each line to be centered on the cloth, then write out the lines, cut each line apart and fold it in half to find the center of each line. Mark the centers, then tape the lines back together, matching centers as shown in the example here.

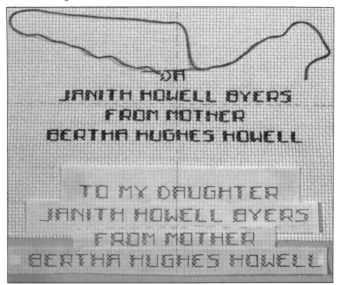

The letters of the label are drawn on graph paper and cut apart to help center each line, then the label is stitched on even-weave cloth from the center out.

3 If the even-weave cloth is to replace a cotton patch in a pieced block, then pre-shrink the fabric and cut it the size of the patch plus seam allowances and center the message on it. However, if the label is not part of a block, you need to know how large to cut the even-weave cloth. Count the number of spaces of the longest line on the graph paper. Divide that number by the size of the canvas. For instance, on the label shown here, the longest line is 75 spaces. The cloth is 11 squares per inch, so divide 75 by 11. The writing area will be nearly 7" wide. When cutting fabric, allow at least two extra inches all the way around plus extra if you are planning to stitch a decorative border.

Sewing a special label to a quilt personalizes it and enhances its value as a keepsake quilt. Shown here are quilt labels made by the different methods described in this chapter and the chapter on Photographs on Fabric. The methods are: 1. Photo on fabric using Picture This™. 2. Stencil using the freezer-wrap method. 3. Letters photocopied on acetate, printed on Inkodye™-treated fabric. 4. Permanent-ink pens. 5. Negative of letters and leaves printed on cyanotype-treated cloth. 6. Juvenile print cut out and appliquéd. 7. Acetate block (enlarged), sun-printed and tea-dyed. 8. Purchased rubber-stamp letters. 9. Hand-quilted message. 10. Rubber stamp.

4 Baste horizontal and vertical lines of thread across the middle of the cloth to help center each line. I prefer to start stitching right in the middle of the cloth, stitching backwards to the beginning of the middle line, then returning to the center and stitching to the end of the line. Then I stitch all the lines above the center and below the center. There is less counting, and my words are sure to be centered.

Using waste canvas

If you prefer to stitch your label on regular-weight cotton, then use waste canvas—also called tear-away canvas—to make your letters evenly spaced. Waste canvas is a stiff, starched, even-weave canvas material available in fabric and craft-supply stores and comes in sizes from 10 to 18 or more squares per inch.

1 Determine the length of each line to be stitched and the size of the canvas as described for even-weave cloth.

2 Baste the canvas to the fabric that is to be embroidered.

3 Find the center of the waste canvas and stitch as described for even-weave cloth, sewing over the canvas threads and through the cloth underneath.

4 Once the stitching is complete, place the entire label in warm water to soften the starch of the

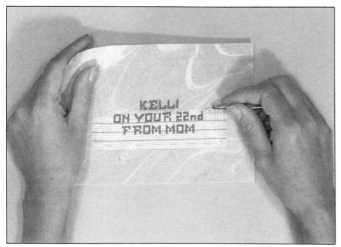

Waste canvas being removed.

canvas. Then you can pull out the canvas threads one by one (tweezers help) until just the stitching remains on the fabric. See the example above.

Other embroidery stitches

The samples here show several other embroidery stitches that are fine for sewing on labels. None of these stitches require even-weave cloth; they can be stitched directly to a cotton label or to the quilt front. You might try writing your name completely in french knots. Or try combining two colors of thread in a woven backstitch as shown. To make your signature fancier, stitch a second time along one edge of all letters.

French knot: Use french knots for all or part of each letter.

Woven backstitch: Follow the outline of each letter with a backstitch, keeping the stitches even lengths. With a contrasting thread, weave around each backstitch with the needle as shown.

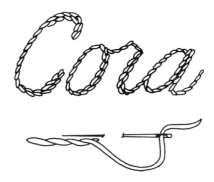

Echo outline: Stitch the word with outline stitching. Add a second row of outline stitches along one edge of each letter.

Stitching without marking

If you want to use your own penmanship for an embroidered label, but you do not want to mark on the fabric, you can stitch directly onto cloth with no marking. Just use your needle and thread like a pencil. Write your message/signature on paper the size you want and keep it handy for reference. Then baste two parallel lines of stitching the height of the small letters to guide you. Embroider your message, keeping the

Outline stitching with no marking.

stitches short so that you can more easily turn curves and corners. Outline stitching is easiest for this method.

Another method is to write your message on tracing or tissue paper with permanent ink (pencil may smudge). Baste the paper to the cloth to be embroidered. Stitch over the drawn message, using an outline stitch, tiny chain stitch, or backstitch. Carefully tear away the paper to leave the stitching.

Embroidery through tissue paper.

Marking

Perhaps you prefer to have the message marked on the fabric to be embroidered. You can write lightly on the fabric with a fine, hard lead in a mechanical pencil or with a wash-out pen, testing first on a scrap of fabric to see if it truly wash-

es out. Or write first on paper, then trace to cloth using a light table, window, or television screen. If you are using a printed alphabet, you should first trace the words in your message on paper to arrange and center them. Then use a light table to trace to cloth for embroidering.

You can make a series of dots to follow when stitching. Pin the tissue paper message to the cloth, then use a mechanical pencil to poke through the lines at short intervals to dot the fabric. Remove the paper and stitch from dot to dot.

Inked signatures

Friendship and album quilts of the mid-1800s were usually signed with india ink. Today quilters have the choice of many products that are suitable for writing on cloth. Many quilt shops now carry the Micron Pigma™ permanent-ink pens. The letters SDK on the side of the pen mean it is permanent on fabric. The pens come in a variety of tip sizes, from .00 (the smallest) to .08. Although .01 is generally sold to quilters, I have found that when given a choice, many people prefer the slightly thicker tip of a .03 or .05 pen. If you cannot find the pen or the correct size, ask your quilt shop or office-supply store to order them. The Pigmas come in blue, brown, red, orange, green, orchid, rose, and black. (*See the source list at the back of the book.*)

Pilot™ permanent felt pens have been used for years on fabric. The pen must have the letters SC-UF on the side to be permanent on fabric. They come in one tip size only, in black, blue (darker than the Pigma), red, green, and orchid. If the tip is allowed to rest on the fabric, the ink may spread, so write quickly or with short strokes, lifting the pen after each stroke.

Niji Stylist™ permanent-ink pens in black and brown have a fine tip, and are excellent for writing on fabric if you want a look similar to the old india-ink pens. Niji FabriColor Superfine Markers™ come in more than 20 colors. The tips are thicker, but the colors are bright and may be just right for the label on a child's quilt. The pen is permanent on all fibers, requires no heat setting, and is virtually fade proof.

Of course, you can still use the time-honored method of writing with permanent india ink (in black, brown, blue, and other colors), using a special fountain pen available in office-supply stores.

Many felt-tipped pens are sold for writing on clothing. Any of these could be used, although they generally have thicker tips that would not be good for delicate writing. The labels will tell whether the ink is for all-cotton or blend fabrics.

When writing directly onto fabric with any of these pens, iron the wrong side of the patch/label onto the shiny side of freezer paper to stabilize it, or tape the fabric to a flat surface. If writing free-hand, you may want to practice on a paper the same size as the patch so you can see how best to center your message. Or write on paper, then trace the writing onto cloth using a light table or window.

Consider adding motifs to your inked label. Small embroidered designs or inked motifs that are incorporated into the signature or message will add design interest and color. See label no. 4 on page 38. Books with traceable designs are available. We offer an alphabet for tracing on page 60 and designs for inking and embroidery on page 61.

Stenciled labels

There was a fad in the mid-1800s for young women to have their signatures made into metal stencils or rubber stamps. These were then used to make calling cards or to write names on the friendship quilts so popular at the time.

Quiltmakers today use these same techniques to add color to their labels. (See label 2 on page 38.) Alphabets and motifs for stenciling are available at craft stores. You can make your own stencils with freezer paper by following these steps.

1 Choose a design or draw your own. Books with quilting motifs are good sources for designs. If your stenciling will be used to add

The label is from the back of the anniversary quilt shown on page 12. The messages were written with various permanent-ink pens described on these pages. Detail at left.

color and interest to a label, nearly any design will work. However, if you wish to write the message within the stenciled design, look for one with an open area to allow for writing.

With the freezer-paper method, the design does not require "bridges" between each cutout area of the design. Whatever portion of the design "falls out" when you cut it can be ironed back in place as shown in the following example.

2 Trace the design on the dull (non-sticky) side of a piece of freezer paper.

41

3 Place the paper on a piece of glass or rotary cutting mat and cut out the design with an X-Acto knife.

4 Iron the freezer paper to the fabric to be stenciled.

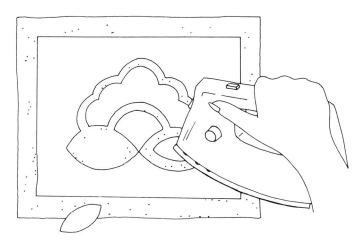

5 Use a water-based or oil-based stenciling paint made for use on fabric. Tape the cloth

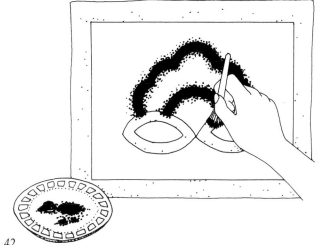

for your label to a surface that won't be harmed by the paint. Use a natural-bristle stenciling brush or cosmetic sponge. Dip the brush or sponge in a tiny amount of the paint and work it into the bristles or sponge. Dab the paint onto the cloth exposed by the freezer-paper cutouts. Do not try to get the paint even throughout. Part of the charm of stenciling is shading. Experiment with adding white or black to the paint to give light and dark areas. Or try a second color to add shading.

6 Allow to dry for 24 hours. Follow the directions that come with the paint, or press for about 30 seconds with a dry iron to heat set the paint.

Rubber stamping

Rubber stamps have been used to stamp names onto cloth for a hundred years. Label 8 on page 38 was made using purchased rubber stamps and textile paints to write the names. The hearts are a printed fabric. Label 10 on page 38 was made by cutting block letters out of rubber-stamp material.

Today there are hundreds of rubber-stamp motifs that can be used to add color to a quilt label. Rubber-stamp alphabets are available from specialty shops. Or you can make your own by carving on a large eraser. One company sells sheets of rubber-stamp material that is rather like thick contact paper. It can be cut easily with scissors or a craft knife, then stuck to a wood block or similar material and used for stamping. Follow these steps to make a stamped label.

1 Purchase or make your rubber stamp(s). (*See the source list at the end of the book.*)

2 Use the same textile paints made for stenciling, or purchase ink made especially for stamping. Place the paint or ink on an ink pad, or brush it

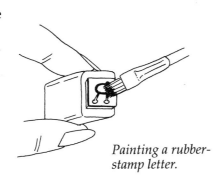

Painting a rubber-stamp letter.

onto the stamp with a brush. Lightly cover the raised portion of the stamp, but do not get any ink on the recessed portions or around the edges of the stamp.

3 Firmly press the stamp onto fabric, keeping the stamp level. Lift it straight up.

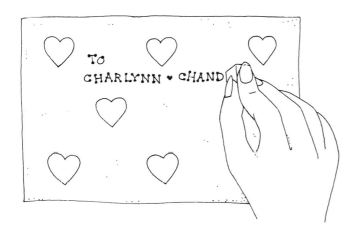

Printing with a rubber stamp.

4 After the ink is dry, heat set it according to the directions given with the ink or paint.

Photos on labels

One method of assuring that no one forgets exactly who made your quilt is to place your own photograph on a label on the back. A photograph of the recipient also is a nice addition. For the label on the back of my sister's 50th-birthday quilt, I added an early black-and-white print of us when we were children and signed it with the nickname she always called me. (See label 1 on page 38.)

To make my son's graduation quilt more personal, I included photos of him when he was 3 years old and when he was 18. The pictures were

part of a pieced block sewn into the quilt top.

One-color copy heat-transfer photographs.

Appliquéd labels

Appliquéd motifs may offer a place to write a message. Perhaps there is appliqué on the quilt top, and you can simply choose a portion of the design to stitch to the lining. If the quilt is all pieced, then you might choose an appliqué pattern that will relate to the quiltmaker or the quilt's recipient. For instance, you might stitch a flower that the person loves, or a heart large enough to contain the written message. The quilt label shown right was made for the back of an Amish wall hanging Marie Kleman made for her grandson. The appliqué shows a woman present-

Appliquéd label with embroidered words.

ing a quilt to a young boy.

For a child's crib quilt that contains a large-scale dinosaur print, I cut out one of the motifs and stitched it to the lining. The dinosaur is waving a balloon that contains the information I want on the quilt. (See label 6 on page 38.)

No matter how complex or simple your label is, the important thing is that you add one to your quilt. It will add immeasurably to the quilt's sentimental value.

Quick Quilts for Special People

Once people realize that you are a quilt-maker, you may be called upon to make a quilt for someone's anniversary, birthday, wedding, or other family occasion. There may be time to produce a quilt such as the family heirlooms shown in other chapters of this book. However, sometimes you may feel the need to make a quilt that takes less of your time. The quilts in this chapter are all special in that they are made with love to honor a person, but none of them takes very long to make.

A 50th wedding anniversary prompted the making of the quilt shown on this page. I needed a simple-to-piece block that would allow plenty of room for messages, because I knew my family would want to say a lot about my parents, Bertha and Ray Howell. I used a simple Album block design

and placed the blocks in a simple setting. The wedding couple's photograph in the center is printed on fabric. (For directions, see the chapter about transferring photographs to fabric.) The muslin patches for the Howell quilt were signed with permanent-ink pens at two large family reunions. Then the blocks were pieced. When I made a similar quilt, shown on page 7, for my in-laws' 50th wedding anniversary, I wanted the quilt to be finished for their anniversary celebration. I mailed paper patches to family and friends and asked for written messages. When they were mailed back, I traced the messages and signatures to fabric using a light box and a permanent-ink pen.

Signature quilts such as these are a good choice for a special-occasion quilt made to celebrate an anniversary, important birthday, or retirement. The blocks

"Happy Golden Anniversary," 54" x 78", made by the author for her parents' wedding anniversary. The photograph is a color-copy heat transfer.

are easy to piece and include a generous space for messages. This type of quilt allows many people to feel a part of the quilt's making, and will be cherished by the recipient.

Part of the fun of making a signature quilt with this Album block is playing with the way blocks are set together. Compare the quilt here with the one on page 7. These blocks can be set in the same arrangements as you would for Log Cabin blocks, such as Barn Raising and Straight Furrows.

There are many traditional patterns associated with signature quilts, including several different Album blocks, Chimney Sweep, Memory Block, and others. But any pattern with space for a signature can be used. Look for blocks with a square or rectangular patch in the center. Even a block that at first glance does not seem suitable might be turned into a signature block by adding a patch of plain fabric somewhere in the block.

Organizing a family signature quilt

If, as in many families, your relatives and friends are scattered in several states and even countries, organizing a family signature quilt takes some time and effort. Here are a few hints to make the task more successful.

▲ Decide first if the project is a one-person effort or if there are other family members who can help you. Even if you do all the sewing, other members can handle the task of corresponding, mailing the blocks, tracing and inking signatures or embroidering them. Perhaps other family members can help you piece the blocks and do the quilting.

▲ Decide whose names are to be included on the quilt. Be prepared to receive fewer or more signatures than planned. Be flexible with your design to accommodate the number that are returned. When I mailed paper patches to relatives with the note, "Copy as needed and hand out to others," I received about two dozen more signatures than I had planned for. I had to double up names on some blocks.

▲ Choose a block size based on the number of signatures you hope to include. If you expect a hundred names, then a 10" block with one name per block would make a quilt too large to be usable. Often these kinds of quilts are treasured and not used on a bed. If it is to be a wall

hanging, keep in mind the home where it will be displayed. If there is no large empty wall, then keep the blocks small.

▲ You can mail the cloth patches or pieced blocks and a permanent-ink pen to each family. If sending the patches, be sure to mark the seam line so no one writes too close to the edge. Iron the patch or pieced block to freezer paper to stabilize it for writing. Include a scrap of fabric for writing practice. Suggest that the signers write the message out first on a piece of paper the size of the finished patch so they can see how to center their message before writing on fabric.

▲ Instead of sending the cloth, you can send patches drawn on paper the size of the finished patch. Ask people to sign the paper with a ball-point pen. (This does not have to be permanent.) Then you can trace the signatures onto cloth using a light table or window. This allows you to center each message, combine more than one signature on a block, or add decorative motifs as desired. This method allows more flexibility and surer success, but means more work for you.

▲ Send a letter explaining the project, who it is for, and what the signers have to do. Give specific directions for signing. Include any of the following that you wish to be on the quilt: Request just signatures or signatures plus messages. Each person signs his/her block, or several people in a family can sign the same block. Messages could be either printed or written. Signatures could be written. Full names or just first names could be used. The person's relationship to the quilt recipient could be made clear. Children can draw a picture, or parents can sign for them. You may think of other criteria for signing the patches.

▲ Set a specific completion date so that everyone knows exactly when the signatures are to be returned to you. Give people a few weeks from the time they receive the material. This deadline should be set several weeks in advance of when you really need the signatures.

▲ Send a stamped, self-addressed envelope large enough to accommodate the blocks or paper patches.

▲ Be sure to let all contributors know if the quilt is to be a secret!

The addition of inked or stenciled motifs on each signature patch is a way of personalizing a signature quilt even more. Also, if some people write long messages and others simply sign a name, the motifs can fill the emptier patches nicely. Each person who signs may design his or her own motif, perhaps based on a hobby or interest. If there is an artist in your family, enlist his or her help in designing motifs. The designs could be inked onto the patches before they are handed out for signing so that the signatures will be integrated with the designs, or you could add them later to fill empty-looking blocks. On page 61 are several motifs that can be inked or embroidered to enhance your signature blocks.

Sun-print signature quilt

One method of making a signature quilt that does not require much sewing time is to use sun-printed mini-quilt blocks that are signed, then stitched with sashing to make a wall quilt for the lucky recipient. The black-and-white block drawings on pages 58 and 59 have been designed especially for this technique. Follow these steps to make a sun-print signature quilt.

1 Take this book with you to a black-and-white copy machine. (Note that the block pages may be copied for your personal use.) Ask the copy machine operator to replace the regular copy

paper with a sheet of acetate (clear plastic) and turn the print setting to dark. Most copy shops will provide the acetate for about 75¢ per sheet. If you have access to a copy machine, you can purchase the acetate at office-supply stores and place it in the machine yourself.

2 Copy the block page to the acetate. If you want blocks that finish larger than 3", then

Blocks copied on acetate and sun printed.

have the copy enlarged to the size desired, if the machine has the capability to enlarge. (If the page is enlarged 150% the blocks will finish 4½".)

3 Use the acetate copy like a negative to print the blocks onto fabric. Follow directions for printing on fabric with cyanotype or Kwik Print™ given in the chapter on photographs on fabric. After printing, the blocks can be turned brown, if desired, following directions on page 27.

If you wish to design your own blocks or images for sun printing, you can draw directly on acetate with india ink. Remember that whatever is black on the acetate will print white on the cloth, so blacken that space on the acetate that will later be used for people to write on.

4 Once you have printed all the blocks you need, cut them apart on the dotted lines and have them signed. Simple sashing strips between blocks add to the beauty of the quilt. Since the blocks are small, you only need to quilt around each square.

"Best Wishes," 24" x 24", made for Carol Crowley by Louise O. Townsend and Vivian Ritter. Patterns for some of the blocks are on pages 58-59. A special signature quilt can be an ideal way of honoring a friend or a relative.

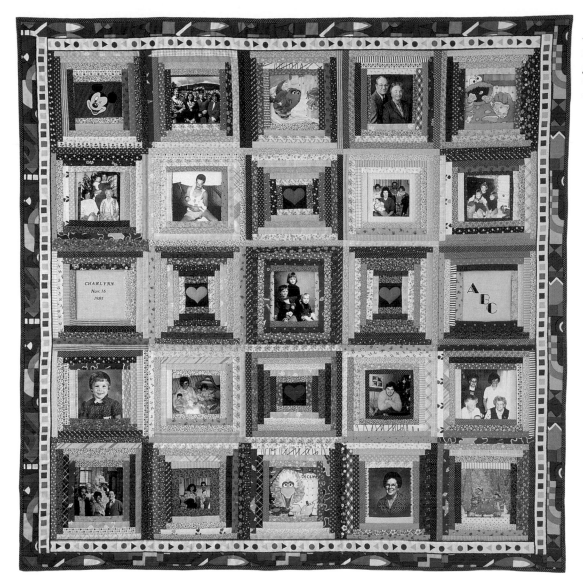

Pop-out picture Log Cabin

As quiltmakers we want to pass on our love of quilts, and one way to do that is to give a quilt that a child can call her or his own–a quilt to be used and loved. Quilts that are easy to make yet are personal in some way make excellent baby and birthday gifts.

A learning quilt, shown above, has spaces for the child to place photos, artwork, pictures from magazines, or whatever strikes his fancy. This idea is also fun for an older child. I made my daughter a wall quilt for her college dorm room (shown on page 49). She updates pictures of family and friends whenever she likes. The center of each Log Cabin block is a square of muslin or printed fabric. The first round of "logs" is made with a folded flap that allows the insertion of cardboard squares that have been covered with pictures. The cardboard inserts can be removed to wash the quilt, and they can be changed whenever the child wants new pictures on the quilt. Things that could be used in the centers include:

▲ color photocopies of photographs or the original photo glued to cardboard

▲ color photocopies of characters in favorite books (If the copy machine operator questions you, explain that it is for personal use only, to be placed on a quilt. Generally they will agree that this is "fair use" of copyrighted material.)

▲ the child's own artwork

▲ your own printing, or press-type letters with the child's name, birth date, ABC's, numbers, other family members' names

▲ pictures cut from magazines of animals or other interests of the child

Instructions for making a Log Cabin quilt with pop-out pictures are on page 62.

Photo gallery Log Cabin

Another Log Cabin variation is shown below. The center of each block is a color-copy heat-transfer photograph. (See the chapter on photographs on fabric for instructions.) The quilt

"The Photo Gallery," 48" x 40", shown in color on page 30.

has black-and-white as well as color photographs. Some are contemporary; some were taken nearly 50 years ago.

The Log Cabin block allows different-sized photographs to be used while the overall Log Cabin design is retained. As with any Log Cabin quilt, there are numerous setting designs possible. Because the photographs are stitched into the blocks, the block arrangements should be determined first so the photographs will be upright when blocks are stitched together later. Instructions for making a similar quilt are on page 64.

Birthday quilt

Everyone is pleased when they are given a quilt with their picture on it. The little quilt shown on page 49 has the child's photograph printed on fabric using a color-copy heat transfer on fabric, as explained on page 29. The simple piecing around the photograph is made interesting with a juvenile print. The child's name and birth date are printed with rubber-stamp alphabet letters and textile paint, and the hearts are stenciled.

This quilt could be given to the family soon after the child is born, using the hospital's

newborn photograph. Or you might wait until the child's first birthday and use a later photograph.

Crayon quilt

Haven't we all papered the front of our refrigerators with drawings from the little ones in our families? Why not keep some of those special images in a more permanent manner? A quilt that uses children's drawings for blocks can be a very special gift, either for the child or for a lucky relative. It can even be a fun gift for a teenager, who will realize that you've cared enough to keep his or her childhood drawings all these years. Or how about a crib quilt for a new mother that has *her* early artwork on it?

Unless you have an exceptional artist in the family, most children's drawings don't have recognizable forms before the child is three or four. (One block of squiggles and circles may be enough on a quilt.) An interesting quilt might be one that uses drawings by several children of different ages. The one shown on the opposite page uses the drawings from two children drawn over a period of four years, so the pictures show their changing levels of ability.

Materials: Crayons made specifically for drawing on fabric are preferred. After being heat set, they are permanent. The colors will not fade and can be washed gently.

▲ Crayola™ Craft Heat Transfer Fabric Crayons come in a box of eight colors and are to be used on polyester or synthetic fabrics. The directions say to draw with the crayons on paper, then iron the image onto the cloth. This makes a reversed image, so lettering will not work. The colors come out somewhat muted and soft looking. I have found that you can draw directly on the fabric and heat set it by placing a paper towel on the picture, and ironing with a hot, dry iron for about 30 seconds. The image is brighter and just as permanent, and there is no problem with backwards letters.

▲ Pentel™ Dyeing Pastels come in sets of 15 colors and give a bright image on cotton fabric. The colors are drawn directly on the fabric, then are heat set with an iron.

▲ Any pens made for writing on fabric can be used. The Niji™ FabriColor Superfine Markers come in many bright colors, but they are purchased individually and are more expensive than either of the other two. See the material on

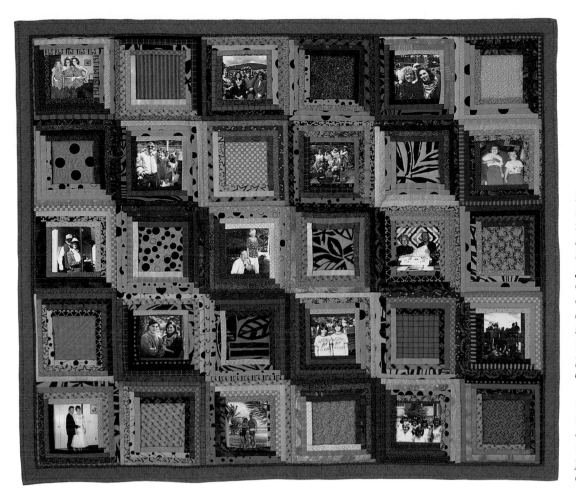

Left, "Tropical Picture Show," 50" x 42", made by the author for her daughter's 22nd birthday. The photographs are regular color copies glued to cardboard that can be easily removed. See a similar pop-out picture Log Cabin on page 47. Directions are on page 62.

Below, "Happy Birthday, Gramma," 34" x 34", made by the author. Directions for this quilt are on the opposite page.

"Birthday Quilt," 24" x 24", made with a color-copy heat-transfer photo by the author. Directions are opposite.

page 40 for a description of other pens suitable for writing on fabric.

Drawing on cloth: Wash and iron the cloth. Cut into blocks of desired size; make more than you will need to allow for some experimentation. Tape a block to a table or iron it to the shiny side of freezer paper to stabilize. Since the block will be stitched into a quilt, allow for seams; use masking tape around the edges so the child will not draw within the seam allowances.

Let the child know that you have plenty of fabric squares so he or she knows that there is more than one opportunity to draw a "good" picture. If using the Pentel crayons, they can be washed out of the fabric before the colors are heat set. Encourage the child to write his or her name and age on the picture.

Drawing on paper: If this is a quilt made "long distance," it may be easier to have the children send pictures drawn on paper squares the size of the finished block, then trace the images to cloth yourself. Or if you are using pictures drawn over a period of time, this is the method to use. Once you have the drawings you want to use, tape a fabric square over the paper drawing. Using a light table, television screen, or window, trace over the drawing line for line, keeping the colors as close to the original as possible. If there is no signature or age on the drawing, add that in block lettering.

The drawings look best when separated with sashing. Or follow directions for setting blocks together as described on the opposite page. If you only have a few drawings, not enough for an entire quilt, make pieced blocks as fillers around the drawings.

Quilts made for a specific occasion such as an anniversary or birthday need not take weeks to make to be special to the recipient. By making it personal with written messages, photographs, or a special label, you can turn even the simplest quilt into a keepsake quilt.

Patterns and Projects

Family keepsake quilts are intrinsically one-of-a-kind quilts. The patterns and projects given on the following pages are to help get you started on designing a family quilt that will be as individual as your family is.

There are many fine books available that describe in detail how to make a quilt from start to finish, so there seems no need to repeat that information here. For your reference, there is a list of books on the inside back cover of this one.

How to make a quilt with various-sized blocks

If you make a family quilt that results in blocks of various sizes, there are several ways of setting these blocks together to make a unified and successful quilt.

Framed blocks

A simple method for stitching together blocks of different sizes is by framing each block to make them all the same size. Use mitered corners or butted corners for the frames. If a block is extra small, you may prefer to use more than one fabric for the frame.

Mitered corners

Butted corners

Simple pieced sashing

This type of sashing can be seen on the quilt on page 10 and on the back-cover quilt.

The dimensions of the *finished* blocks (with no seam allowances added) should be in whole inches, such as 7" x 10". If you are cutting a back-

ground square for appliqué, be sure to add ¼" seam allowances, so the *cut* size would be 7½" x 10½".

Draw each finished block size on quarter-inch graph paper, having one square equal one inch. Cut the blocks out and arrange them on a sheet of graph paper, leaving spaces between

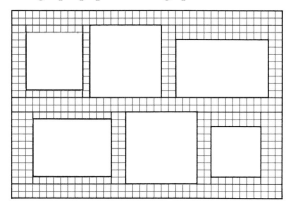

them that will represent the pieced sashing. Once you have a composition that is balanced and pleasing, count the number of squares between blocks to see how wide to make each sash.

Cut 1½" squares out of sashing fabrics. Sew these squares to each block as needed so that blocks can be sewn together easily in straight seams.

Log Cabin frame:

The directions for using Log Cabin piecing around each block are given on page 64.

Modular unit set

Make each block's finished measurement a multiple of a certain number such as 4": the blocks could be 4" x 4", 4" x 8", 8" x 12", etc. All blocks can then be joined like a puzzle. Use plain blocks to fill in where needed.

Folk art family tree

If you enjoy machine or hand appliqué, here is a design idea that makes a charming family tree quilt. These patterns, adapted from Connie Nordstrom's quilt shown on page 10, will enable you to design your own family tree quilt, changing the people to fit your family members. There are hair variations and interchangeable faces, plus a house, car, pets, and trees. Look at Connie's quilt for other ideas you may wish to try. Your embellishments and variations will truly make it a "folk-art" expression.

Working on graph paper, decide on the number and size of your square and rectangular blocks. Plan to piece the blocks together using one of the settings described on the previous page.

Plan clothing in the colors that the person typically wears. Include items relating to hobbies, career, sports, and so forth for each person.

To make templates, trace the pattern pieces and adhere them to cardboard. Cut out templates. For hand appliqué, place templates face up on right side of fabric and mark around them. Cut the fabric patch 3/16" outside marked lines. Turn under the edges of the patch just inside the marked lines; baste. It is not necessary to turn under edges that will be covered by other patches. *Or*, follow directions on page 19 for working with the small appliquéd shapes. Position, pin, and blindstitch the patches on the background fabric from the lowest layer of patches to the uppermost layer.

For machine appliqué, mark around the templates as described above. Cut fabric patches on marked lines. Position, pin, and zigzag stitch patches to background blocks.

Use embroidery or ink to add features and other details.

Satin Stitch

Outline Stitch   *Lazy Daisy Stitch*

53

Little house quilt

If you would like to make a quilt depicting family relationships, this pieced pattern may be just what you are looking for. The three family tree quilts shown on pages 14 and 15 were made using the patterns on the following three pages. Each quilt contains a different number of houses based on the number of families being represented on the quilt. When you read the text on those pages, you will see how the family relationships were depicted on those quilts.

If you wish to design a similar quilt for your family tree, photocopy this page and cut apart the blocks on the dark lines. Have the blocks enlarged if you wish.

Assign a miniature house to each family you plan to include, writing initials or a name on the house to help you keep track. You may wish to use a house with the same number of windows as the number of children in the family. If there are more than four children, then windows can be split in half or quarters with embroidered lines.

Arrange the mini-blocks in a square, or in a vertical or horizontal rectangle as shown here, placing the houses of sons and daughters below or to the side of their parents' houses, or in whatever arrangement seems logical. If there are too many houses, you may need to eliminate some by placing more names on one block. (A child could have her or his own house or the name could be on a window of the parents' house.) Embroider or ink messages on

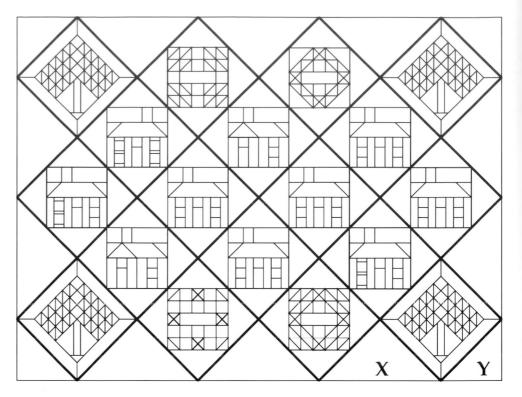

the blocks given on page 57, and use these message blocks and trees as "fillers" and to balance the overall design. You may wish to include plain blocks for a label or photograph printed on fabric.

The house block is 6" square. After adding N patches to each edge, the house block has a diagonal measure of 12". You can determine how large your quilt will be by counting the number of blocks across one row. Multiply that number by 12". The quilt shown above would be 48" wide and 36" high without borders.

Once you have determined the number of houses and filler blocks that you need, follow the diagrams on the following pages to make the blocks. Join blocks and X and Y edge patches in diagonal rows; join rows. Add borders as desired.

This page may be photocopied for personal use.

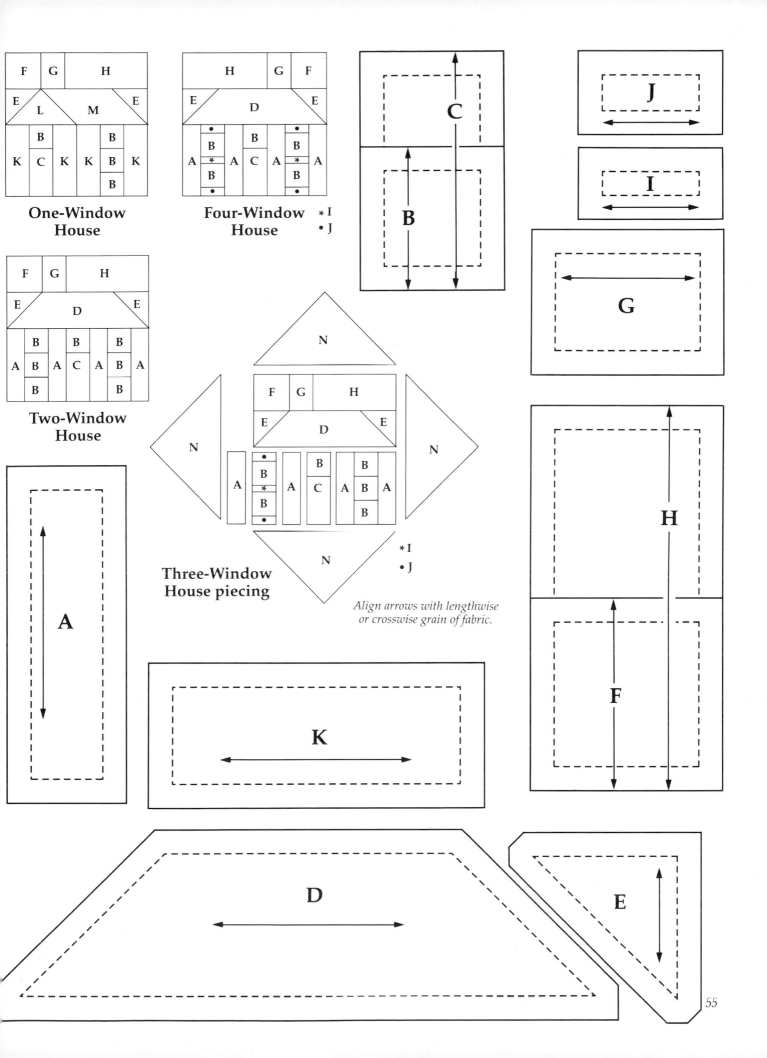

One-Window House

Four-Window House *I • J

Two-Window House

Three-Window House piecing *I • J

Align arrows with lengthwise or crosswise grain of fabric.

Tree block

This pattern makes an 8½" tree block. The diagonal measure of the block is 12", the same size as the house block after N patches are sewn on. Refer to the piecing diagram here to make as many trees as you need for your design. By changing the colors of the tree patches, you can make the trees appear to be growing in different seasons. One or two red Q patches will look like cardinals sitting in the tree.

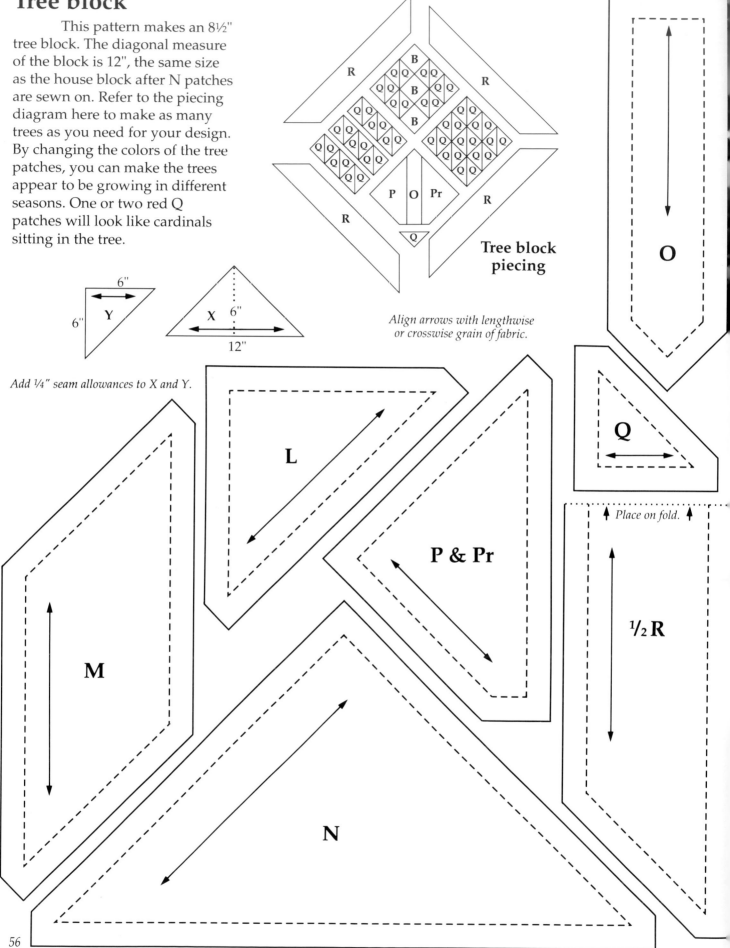

Tree block piecing

Align arrows with lengthwise or crosswise grain of fabric.

Add ¼" seam allowances to X and Y.

Place on fold.

Message blocks

The four pieced blocks given here are shown on the quilt on page 15. They can be used as "fillers" in your house quilt where needed. By changing where light- and dark-value fabrics are used, an abundance of design variations can be made.

Use the S patch for messages. Write or embroider information about the families on the quilt, including countries of origin, states where the members have lived, sentimental sayings, and so on. See the chapter on special labels for more ideas. Don't forget to write on the quilt (either on a message block or a label on the lining) information about who made the quilt, when and where it was made, and for what occasion.

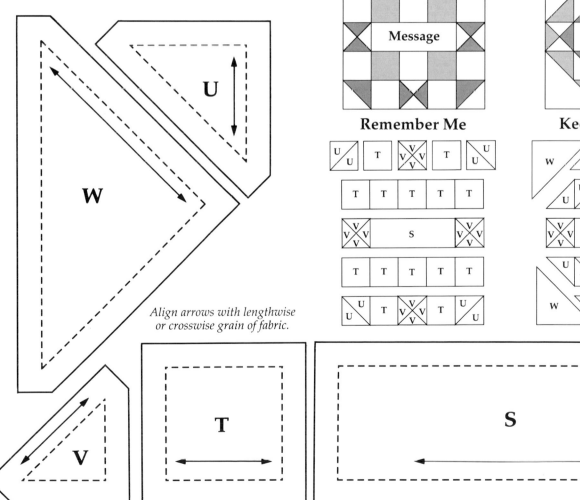

Align arrows with lengthwise or crosswise grain of fabric.

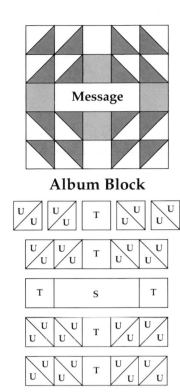

Memory Block

Album Block

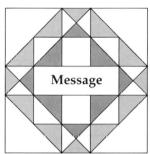

Remember Me

Keepsake Block

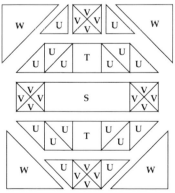

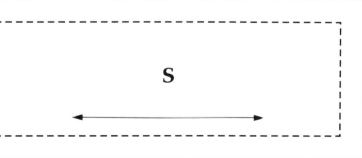

Sun print signature blocks

The eight block motifs given on these two pages were used to make the signature quilt shown on page 46. The blocks are printed here as negatives. What is black will print light, leaving a center space for signatures. Follow steps 1 and 2 on page 46 to print these pages onto acetate. The blocks also can be enlarged when they are printed onto acetate if you wish to print larger quilt blocks. The acetate blocks can be cut apart for individual sun printing, or they can be printed as given here. (Each group of four will fit onto an 8" square of treated sun-print fabric.)

Prepare the fabric for sun printing as described on page 24 for cyanotype or page 28 for Kwik Print™. Layer the fabric and acetate blocks as described on page 26. Place the layered "sand-

This page may be photocopied for personal use.

wich" outside and print in the sun. When printed, rinse the fabric as described for the method you are using.

The dotted lines around the blocks will print on the cloth so that the blocks can be cut apart, leaving 1/4" seam allowances. Add signatures in the open spaces in the centers of the blocks. Join the blocks with or without sashing to make your quilt the desired size.

As well, individual blocks can be used for labels on backs of quilts. Another idea is to make a sun print from one of these blocks, then quilt it with filler and backing to make a charming name tag. You may think of other uses for these miniature blocks.

Alphabets

Any quilt is enhanced with a label that describes who made it and when. If you wish to stitch an embroidered label, here are two small alphabets and numbers that work well on even-weave fabric and waste canvas. Read the directions for embroidered labels on pages 36-39 for information on size of canvas to use, centering words, and stitch diagrams.

If you prefer to ink your message and signature, the alphabet on the bottom of the page can be used. To make the letters larger, have this page enlarged to the desired size on a photocopy machine. Place a piece of tracing paper over the alphabet and trace the letters with any dark pen in the order needed to write your message. If lines are not centered to your satisfaction, cut the paper apart and tape it back together to center. Once the entire message is written on paper, tape it to a light box, TV screen, or window. Place the fabric for your label over the words and trace with permanent-ink pen on the cloth.

Cross Stitch Alphabet

Backstitch Alphabet

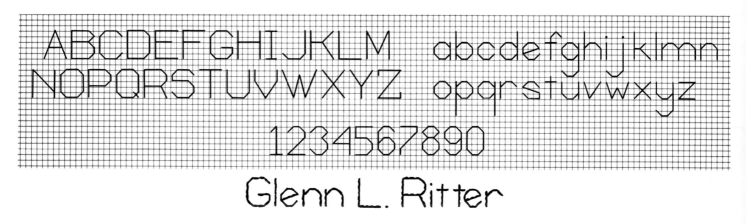

Glenn L. Ritter

Handwritten Alphabet

ABCDEFGGHIJKLMNO
PQRSTUVWXYZ
abcdefghijklmnopqrstuvwxyz
1234567890
Glenn L. Ritter

Information about kinds of pens to use is on page 40.

Motifs to embroider and ink

Signature blocks and labels can be enhanced with these motifs. Refer to page 40 for information about using permanent-ink pens to ink the motifs. Or, if you prefer, use embroidery to add the motifs to your quilts.

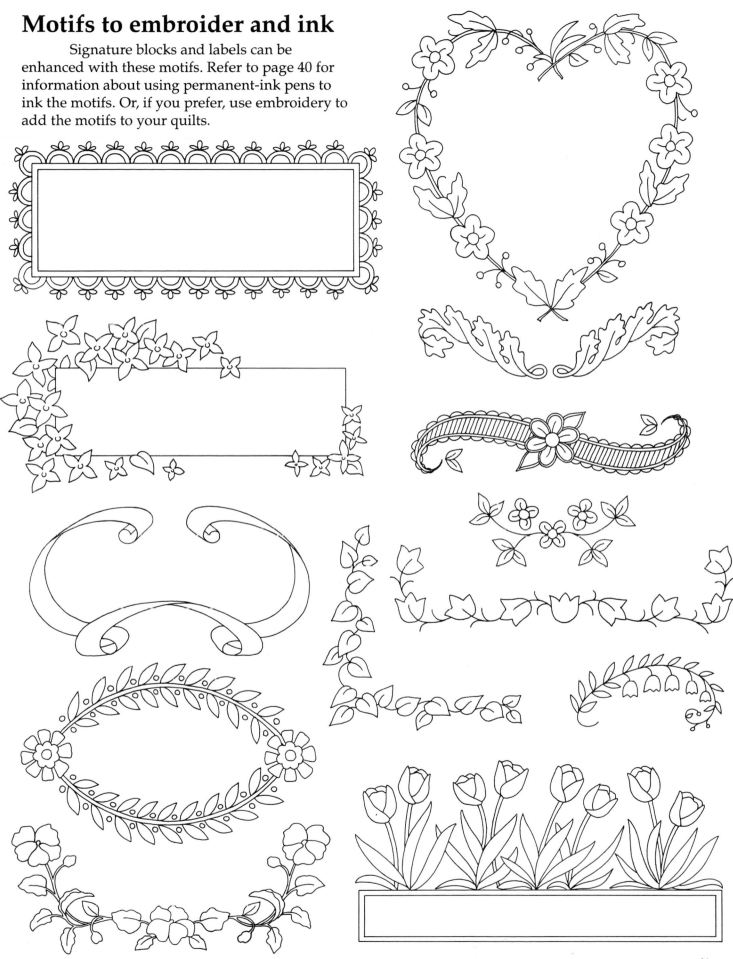

This page may be photocopied for personal use.

Pop-out picture Log Cabin

Imagine how much fun a child or teen would have changing the pictures and photographs in the centers of the blocks in their Log Cabin Quilt. A picture of a new friend or member of the family could be added easily to this ever-changing picture show. As the child's art abilities grow, the new works of art can replace the old ones. This Log Cabin pattern (two variations are shown on pages 47 and 49) allows the insertion of photographs, drawings, and other pictures that have been glued to a stiffener such as cardboard. The pictures pop out easily so the quilt can be washed.

Assembly

1 Plan your design on paper and determine how many 8" blocks you need, or follow one of the quilt designs shown here. Referring to the block diagrams on the bottom of the opposite page, determine whether you need Sunshine and Shadow blocks or Courthouse Steps blocks or a combination of the two types. In the child's quilt on page 47 (the quilt diagram is shown at right), there are four Courthouse Steps blocks made with blue and light scrap strips, with small centers made from printed heart fabric. The 16 outer blocks are Courthouse Steps blocks made with a variety of colors. There are four blocks that are made with only light strips to allow the blue star to be more apparent. The center block is made of red strips only.

The teen's "Tropical Picture Show" quilt on page 49 is made with Sunshine and Shadow blocks–half with blue/aqua strips, half with purple/pink strips. See the block arrangement on the opposite page.

2 For each block, cut a center patch that is 5½" square. This measure *includes* ¼" seam allowances. If you plan to have a picture in each block, then this square can be made of muslin or any fabric you have on hand. However, if you wish some of the fabric centers to show, then make the centers from coordinating fabrics.

3 The first round of "logs" is made from strips that are folded and stitched in place to form a fabric frame that holds the pictures in place. Cut 2 dark strips and 2 light strips each 1½" wide and 5½" long for the first round. With *wrong* sides

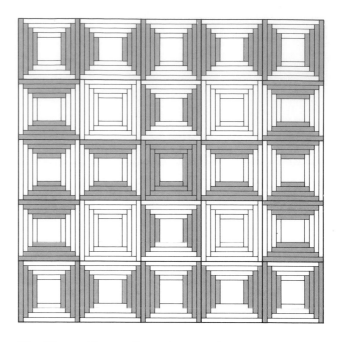

The Picture Show quilt setting. See the quilt on page 47.

together, fold the 1½" strips in half lengthwise and press.

4 Referring to the figure below, align raw edges of a folded strip with the top edge of a 5½" center square. Align another strip with the bottom edge. (Note the differences in the placement of light and dark strips between Courthouse Steps and Sunshine and Shadow blocks.) Stitch in a ¼" seam. Do *not* press strips *away* from the center square. They remain in place as sewn.

Courthouse Steps	Sunshine and Shadow

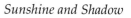

 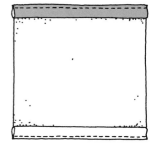

5 Repeat for the sides. Again, do *not* press strips away from the center. They remain in place.

Courthouse Steps	Sunshine and Shadow

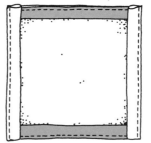 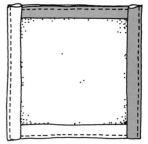

6 To add the second round of strips, for a Sunshine and Shadow block cut 1 light and 1 dark strip each 1" x 5½"; cut 1 light and 1 dark strip each 1" x 6½". For a Courthouse Steps block cut 2 dark strips 1" x 5½" and 2 light strips 1" x 6½". These strips do not get folded. Referring to the figures below, align the raw edge of a 5½" strip with the top edge of the block. (Again, follow diagrams for either Courthouse Steps or Sunshine and Shadow for light/dark placement.) Stitch in a ¼" seam, sewing through all layers. Repeat for the bottom. Press strips *away* from the block.

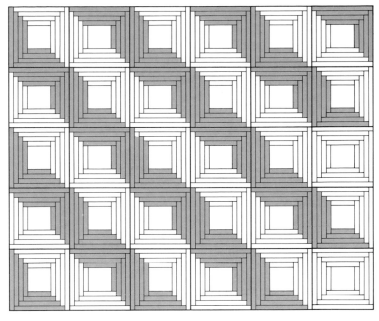

Tropical Picture Show quilt setting. See the quilt on page 49.

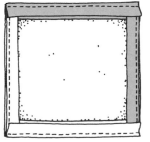

Courthouse Steps   *Sunshine and Shadow*

7 Stitch 6½" strips to side edges and press away from the block.

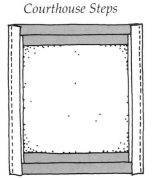

Courthouse Steps   *Sunshine and Shadow*

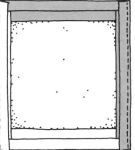

8 Cut the next round of strips 1" x 6½" and 1" x 7½" and sew to the block. Cut strips for the final round 1" x 7½" and 1" x 8½". Sew on these rounds of strips, stitching in a ¼" seam and pressing the strips away from the block. If you wish the block to be larger than 8", continue sewing on strips until the block is the desired size. Make as many blocks as needed for your design.

9 Join blocks in rows and join rows. Layer quilt lining, batting, and top. Quilt in-the-ditch around blocks. Bind to finish.

10 Cut cardboard 4⅞" square or slightly smaller for easy insertion. Glue a photograph or another kind of picture on the cardboard square. If the picture seems too small for the block opening, glue fabric or construction paper to the cardboard, then center and glue the picture on the cardboard. Insert as many pop-out pictures as you need for your quilt. The inserts are easy to pop in and out for an ever-changing display of your child's interests.

Courthouse Steps   *Sunshine and Shadow*

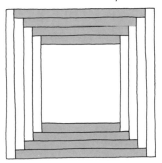
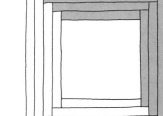

Photo gallery Log Cabin

Several of the quilts shown on the previous pages as well as the memory quilt shown on the back cover are made with blocks of varying sizes. This method of making Log Cabin blocks allows you to use centers of varying sizes to make a quilt that looks unified.

The quilt shown on page 30 uses color-copy heat transfers applied to fabric in the centers of the Log Cabin blocks. The finished size of each block is 8" square, but the inside center patch of each block is a different size, depending on the size of the photograph. To allow for this variation, each block may use a different number of "logs." The photos are permanently sewn in place.

The directions here are for a quilt that uses photos printed on fabric in the center, but a similar quilt could be made with any type of center, including appliquéd memory blocks like those shown on the back-cover quilt, folk art family tree blocks, or children's drawings. The blocks for these quilts might need to be larger than 8" to accommodate the larger centers. Simply add more logs until blocks are the desired size.

Assembly

1 Cut each fabric photo to measure whole inches or half inches–for instance, 3½" x 4" or 5½" x 4½". (The measurements should *include* ¼" seam allowances.)

2 The blocks can be sewn together in any Log Cabin set. We show three settings on these pages. Referring to the block diagrams on the previous page, decide whether your overall design requires Sunshine and Shadow blocks or Courthouse Steps blocks. Plan your setting before

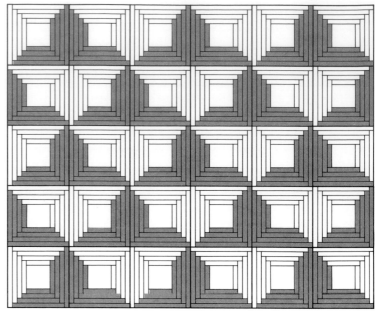

Photo Gallery Log Cabin setting. See the quilt on page 30.

you sew the blocks because once the photographs are sewn in place, the blocks cannot be rotated.

3 Cut all strips 1" wide. The length of the strips will range in size from your smallest photograph to 8½" long. You may prefer to cut all the strips as long as you can, then cut the lengths as needed.

4 Add strips to the edges of a fabric photo to make the photo square. In the figures below, the strips shown in gray indicate where additional strips have been added to square the photos. Then sew on additional strips in the regular Log Cabin fashion to make a block that is 8½" square from raw edge to raw edge.

5 Sew blocks in rows and join rows. Layer lining, batting, and quilt top; baste. Quilt in-the-ditch around blocks and bind to finish.

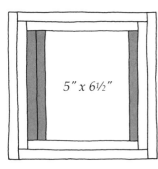
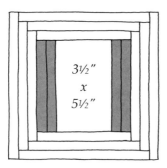
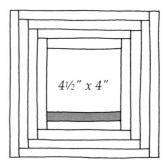
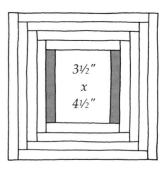

5" x 6½"

3½" x 5½"

4½" x 4"

3½" x 4½"

Blocks with strips added to square the centers. The numbers refer to the cut sizes of the centers.

Sources

Sources for materials

BLUEPRINTS-PRINTABLES
1504 #7 Industrial Way (K.Q.)
Belmont, CA 94002
Sun print (cyanotype) kits with 8" cotton squares ready for printing. Send self-addressed stamped envelope (S.A.S.E.) for price list.

Cabin Fever Calicoes
PO Box 550106
Atlanta, GA 30355
404/873-5094
Pigma pens, phrase books, disappearing (waste) canvas. Catalog $2.

Cerulean Blue, Ltd.
PO Box 21168
Seattle, WA 98111-3168
206/323-8600
Pentel Dyeing Pastels, Niji FabriColor Superfine Markers, Crayola Fabric Crayons, Sure-Stamp rubber stamp material, textile paints, Inkodye for one-color photos. Catalog $4.50.

Crafter's Gallery
Box 4169
Huntington Station, NY 11746
Picture This. Write for price.

Donnelly Offset Negatives
269 Central Avenue
Rochester, NY 14605
716/232-3996
Half-tone negatives. Send a long S.A.S.E. for price list.

Fabric Fotos
3801 Olsen #3
Amarillo, TX 79108
806/359-8241
Color-copy heat transfers printed on fabric. Send S.A.S.E. for price list.

Gramma's Graphics, Inc.
20 Birling Gap, Dept. LPUB-Z1
Fairport, NY 14450
Chemistry for cyanotype sun prints. Send $1 plus a long S.A.S.E. for brochure.

INKADINKADOO
76 South St. (Dept. Q)
Boston, MA 02111
617/426-3458
Custom-made rubber stamps, alphabets. Free catalog.

Light Impressions
439 Monroe Ave.
Rochester, NY 14607-3717
Kwik Print chemicals for one-color photos on fabric. Write for price list.

photoTextiles
PO Box 3063
Bloomington, IN 47402-3063
800/388-3961
Color-copy heat transfers. Write for price list.

Quilts & Other Comforts
PO Box 394
Wheatridge, CO 80034-0394
Quilt books, magazines, patterns, sun-print kits, fabrics, supplies, permanent-ink pens. Free catalog.

Vermont Patchworks
Box 229, Dept. K.F.Q.
Shrewsbury, VT 05738
800/451-4044
Pictures to Fabric gel, permanent-ink pens, Transfer Magic.

Wallflower Designs
1573 Millersville Rd.
Millersville, MD 21108
301/923-6895
Printed quilt labels, book of quotes. Catalog $1.50.

Sources for patterns

Barbara Brackman
500 Louisiana Ave.
Lawrence, KS 66044
An Encyclopedia of Pieced Quilt Patterns *book
with names and drawings of traditional blocks. Write
for price.*

Dover Publications, Inc.
31 East 2nd St.
Mineola, NY 11501
*Many books with designs for stenciling and inking;
embroidered alphabets. Free catalog.*

Quilter's Newsletter Magazine
6700 W. 44th Avenue
Wheatridge, CO 80034-0394
*Regularly features collections of state block patterns.
Write for information.*

Sources for more keepsake quilt photographs

Bresenhan, Karoline Patterson and Nancy
O'Bryant Puentes. *Lone Stars: A Legacy of Texas
Quilts, 1836-1936.* Austin: University of Texas
Press, 1986.

Cleveland, Richard and Donna Bister. *Plain and
Fancy–Vermont's People And Their Quilts As A
Reflection Of America.* San Francisco: The Quilt
Digest Press, 1991.

Crews, Patricia Cox and Ronald C. Naugle.
Nebraska Quilts & Quiltmakers. Lincoln, Nebraska:
University of Nebraska Press, 1991.

The Indiana Quilt Registry Project. *Quilts of
Indiana–Crossroads of Memories.* Bloomington,
Indiana: Indiana University Press, 1991.

Laury, Jean Ray and California Heritage Quilt
Project. *Ho for California!* New York: E.P. Dutton,
1990.

Lipsett, Linda Otto. *Remember Me: Women and
Their Friendship Quilts* (1985); *To Love & To Cherish*
(1989). San Francisco: The Quilt Digest Press.

Twelker, Nancyann Johanson. *Women and Their
Quilts–A Washington State Centennial Tribute.*
Bothell, Washington: That Patchwork Place, 1988.

Woodard, Thos. K. and Blanche Greenstein.
Twentieth Century Quilts 1900-1950. New York:
E. P. Dutton, 1988.